ATLAS
SHRUGGED

Ayn Rand

SPARKNOTES is a registered trademark of SparkNotes LLC.

Spark Publishing
A Division of Barnes & Noble
120 Fifth Avenue
New York, NY 10011
www.sparknotes.com

ISBN-13: 978-1-5866-3821-4
ISBN-10: 1-5866-3821-1

Please submit changes or report errors to www.sparknotes.com/errors.

Printed and bound in the United States

20 19 18 17 16 15 14 13 12 11

INTRODUCTION:
STOPPING TO BUY SPARKNOTES ON A SNOWY EVENING

Whose words these are you *think* you know.
Your paper's due tomorrow, though;
We're glad to see you stopping here
To get some help before you go.

Lost your course? You'll find it here.
Face tests and essays without fear.
Between the words, good grades at stake:
Get great results throughout the year.

Once school bells caused your heart to quake
As teachers circled each mistake.
Use SparkNotes and no longer weep,
Ace every single test you take.

Yes, books are lovely, dark, and deep,
But only what you grasp you keep,
With hours to go before you sleep,
With hours to go before you sleep.

Contents

CONTEXT

A YN RAND WAS BORN ALISSA ROSENBAUM on February 2, 1905, in St. Petersburg, Russia, to an upper-middle-class family. She took an early interest in literature and decided at age nine to become a writer. While still in high school, Rand witnessed the Bolshevik Revolution, which she denounced. When the Communists came to power, Rand's father's pharmacy was nationalized, driving the family to near-starvation. To escape the violence of the revolution, her family moved to the Crimea, where she finished high school. She studied American history in high school and decided that America offered the best example of a free society. Her growing love for the West was fed by the many American films she saw as a teenager and by the works of Victor Hugo, the writer she most admired. After high school, her family returned from the Crimea, and Rand enrolled in the University of Petrograd to study philosophy and history. She graduated in 1924 and then entered the State Institute for Cinema Arts to study screenwriting.

In 1925, Rand obtained a temporary visa to visit relatives in the United States. She intended never to return to her homeland. After living for six months with relatives in Chicago, she obtained an extension of her visa and went to Hollywood to pursue a career as a screenwriter. She took a job as an extra on the set of *The King of Kings*, a Cecil B. DeMille production. A week later, she met Frank O'Connor, whom she married in 1929. The marriage lasted until his death fifty years later.

During her first several years in Hollywood, Rand worked at various occupations. In 1932, she sold her first screenplay, *Red Pawn*, to Universal Studios and had her first stage play, *Night of January 16th*, produced in Hollywood and later on Broadway. She completed her first novel, *We the Living*, in 1933, but was rejected by every American publisher she approached. Finally, in 1936, the Macmillan Company published the book in the United States. The novel was based on her years under Soviet Communism and was strongly criticized by the pro-Communist intelligentsia. She began writing *The Fountainhead* in 1935. As with her previous novel, she had trouble finding a willing publisher. The Bobbs-Merrill Company finally accepted the manuscript in 1943, and, two years later, it became a bestseller through word of mouth. Instantly, Ayn Rand became the champion of individualism.

Rand began writing *Atlas Shrugged* in 1946. The novel was published by Random House in 1957 and became a bestseller despite very negative reviews. *Atlas Shrugged* was her last work of fiction. Rand realized that in order to communicate the full meaning of her philosophy, she would have to identify its principles in nonfiction form, and so for the next twenty-five years she devoted her life to the development and promotion of Objectivism, her philosophy of the ego. In 1958 she founded an institute devoted to teaching her philosophy, which is still active today. She died on March 6, 1982, in her New York City apartment. More than twenty million copies of her books have been sold.

The events that surrounded Rand's life, notably the rise of Communism in Russia, heavily influenced her work. Her distaste for Communism and collectivism in all forms is apparent throughout *Atlas Shrugged*. Although her earlier novels were criticized for their deeply anti-Communist stance, *Atlas Shrugged* was published at the height of the Cold War, and its message was welcomed by an America that feared and despised Communism. At the end of World War II, even when the totalitarian threat of the Nazis had been eliminated, much of Europe, followed by China, Korea, and Cuba, fell under Communism. Communism, a collectivist system that forces individuals to sacrifice their own interests for the good of the state, threatened the personal and intellectual freedoms Rand considered essential. Although the United States opposed Communism in the Cold War era, many of the collectivist beliefs of Marxism had support among American academics and those who favored an expanded welfare state and greater regulation of private industry. Rand wrote *Atlas Shrugged* in opposition to these views.

As a student of American capitalism, Rand believed that unfettered economic freedom was the factor most responsible for the major achievements of American inventors and businessmen during the nineteenth and early twentieth centuries. *Atlas Shrugged* attempts to demonstrate what might happen to the world if such economic freedom were lost, if emerging collectivist trends were to continue to their logical conclusions. The novel shows in detail the resulting collapse of efficient production and the rise of corruption among businessmen and politicians who look to live off the production of others without producing anything themselves. In *Atlas Shrugged*, the system falls apart to the point that the remaining producers choose to simply withdraw rather than perpetuate the corruption. This withdrawal is the strike at the center of the novel's action. In this strike, the thinkers withdraw their minds to protest the oppression of thought and the forced moral code of self-sacrifice that obligates them to work only to serve the needs of others. Without the minds of these thinkers, society is doomed to utter collapse. For Ayn Rand, the mind is the most important tool for humanity, and reason is its greatest virtue.

PLOT OVERVIEW

N AN ENVIRONMENT OF WORSENING economic conditions, Dagny Taggart, vice president in charge of operations, works to repair Taggart Transcontinental's crumbling Rio Norte Line to service Colorado, the last booming industrial area in the country. Her efforts are hampered by the fact that many of the country's most talented entrepreneurs are retiring and disappearing. The railroad's crisis worsens when the Mexican government nationalizes Taggart's San Sebastian Line. The line had been built to service Francisco d'Anconia's copper mills, but the mills turn out to be worthless. Francisco had been a successful industrialist, and Dagny's lover, but has become a worthless playboy. To solve the railroad's financial problems, Dagny's brother Jim uses political influence to pass legislation that destroys Taggart's only competition in Colorado. Dagny must fix the Rio Norte Line immediately and plans to use Rearden Metal, a new alloy created by Hank Rearden. When confronted about the San Sebastian mines, Francisco tells Dagny he is deliberately destroying d'Anconia Copper. Later he appears at Rearden's anniversary party and, meeting him for the first time, urges Rearden to reject the freeloaders who live off of him.

The State Science Institute issues a denunciation of Rearden metal, and Taggart's stock crashes. Dagny decides to start her own company to rebuild the line, and it is a huge success. Dagny and Rearden become lovers. Together they discover a motor in an abandoned factory that runs on static electricity, and they seek the inventor. The government passes new legislation that cripples industry in Colorado. Ellis Wyatt, an oil industrialist, suddenly disappears after setting fire to his wells. Dagny is forced to cut trains, and the situation worsens. Soon, more industrialists disappear. Dagny believes there is a destroyer at work, taking men away when they are most needed. Francisco visits Rearden and asks him why he remains in business under such repressive conditions. When a fire breaks out and they work together to put it out, Francisco understands Rearden's love for his mills.

Rearden goes on trial for breaking one of the new laws, but refuses to participate in the proceedings, telling the judges they can coerce him by force but he won't help them to convict him. Unwilling to be seen as thugs, they let him go. Economic dictator Wesley

Mouch needs Rearden's cooperation for a new set of socialist laws, and Jim needs economic favors that will keep his ailing railroad running after the collapse of Colorado. Jim appeals to Rearden's wife Lillian, who wants to destroy her husband. She tells him Rearden and Dagny are having an affair, and he uses this information in a trade. The new set of laws, Directive 10-289, is irrational and repressive. It includes a ruling that requires all patents to be signed over to the government. Rearden is blackmailed into signing over his metal to protect Dagny's reputation.

Dagny quits over the new directive and retreats to a mountain lodge. When she learns of a massive accident at the Taggart Tunnel, she returns to her job. She receives a letter from the scientist she had hired to help rebuild the motor, and fears he will be the next target of the destroyer. In an attempt to stop him from disappearing, she follows him in an airplane and crashes in the mountains. When she wakes up, she finds herself in a remote valley where all the retired industrialists are living. They are on strike, calling it a strike of the mind. There, she meets John Galt, who turns out to be both the destroyer and the man who built the motor. She falls in love with him, but she cannot give up her railroad, and she leaves the valley. When she returns to work, she finds that the government has nationalized the railroad industry. Government leaders want her to make a speech reassuring the public about the new laws. She refuses until Lillian comes to blackmail her. On the air, she proudly announces her affair with Rearden and reveals that he has been blackmailed. She warns the country about its repressive government.

With the economy on the verge of collapse, Francisco destroys the rest of his holdings and disappears. The politicians no longer even pretend to work for the public good. Their vast network of influence peddling creates worse chaos, as crops rot waiting for freight trains that are diverted for personal favors. In an attempt to gain control of Francisco's mills, the government stages a riot at Rearden Steel. But the steelworkers organize and fight back, led by Francisco, who has been working undercover at the mills. Francisco saves Rearden's life, then convinces him to join the strike.

Just as the head of state prepares to give a speech on the economic situation, John Galt takes over the airwaves and delivers a lengthy address to the country, laying out the terms of the strike he has organized. In desperation, the government seeks Galt to make him their economic dictator. Dagny inadvertently leads them to him, and they take him prisoner. But Galt refuses to help them, even after he is tortured. Finally, Dagny and the strikers rescue him in an armed confrontation with guards. They return to the valley, where Dagny finally joins the strike. Soon, the country's collapse is complete and the strikers prepare to return.

Character List

Dagny Taggart The novel's protagonist and vice president in charge of operations of Taggart Transcontinental. Dagny is Galt's greatest love and worst enemy. Her brilliant management style and unwavering commitment to the railroad enable her to remain in the world of the "looters"—Rand's word for the people and government agencies that seize property from capitalists—and to keep her railroad running despite the growing chaos. In so doing, she continues to provide the looters with transportation that sustains their system. She mistakenly believes the looters are capable of reason and will understand their mistakes before it is too late. When she realizes the looters are in fact agents of death, she withdraws and is the last to join the strike.

Hank Rearden The greatest of the nation's industrialists, Rearden is a steel baron with an astonishing capacity to produce. He is also Dagny's lover for most of the novel. Rearden represents a threat to the strikers because he continues to fight for his mills and inadvertently props up the looters' regime. His main flaw is his willingness to accept the looters' idea that he is obligated to serve others. When he finally gives up this premise, he sees the looters' system for what it is and joins the strike.

John Galt The man around whom the action of the novel revolves, Galt organizes and leads the strike of the mind. He is simultaneously the destroyer, the inventor of the revolutionary motor, Eddie's mysterious friend, and Dagny's greatest love. Brilliant and perceptive, he is the physical and intellectual representation of man's ideal.

Francisco d'Anconia An enormously wealthy and brilliant industrialist, Francisco is the first to join Galt's strike and the man who pays the highest price for it, losing his first and only love, Dagny. Francisco works as the strike's most active recruiter, focusing much of his attention on Rearden. By pretending to be a worthless playboy, Francisco is able to hide his efforts to destroy d'Anconia copper and thereby keep it out of the hands of the looters.

James Taggart (Jim) Dagny's brother and president of Taggart Transcontinental. An inferior businessman, Jim excels at influence peddling and becomes highly skilled at manipulating the system. Though he claims to be motivated by both personal wealth and public service, his true motive is destruction of the productive. Jim carefully represses the nature of his depravity, but his final encounter with John Galt completely shatters his illusions.

Eddie Willers Dagny's assistant at Taggart and a hard worker dedicated to the preservation of the railroad. Through his friendship with the mysterious track worker in the cafeteria, Eddie unwittingly provides the destroyer with valuable information about Dagny and the railroad.

Lillian Rearden Hank Rearden's lifeless, beautiful wife. Lillian is dominated by a hatred of the good, and her purpose in life is to destroy her husband. Unlike Jim, who shares her need for destruction but deludes himself that he has other motivations, Lillian is honest with herself about her goals.

Ellis Wyatt An oil tycoon who sparks the growth of Colorado's industry through his innovations. When the government burdens Colorado with impossible regulations and demands, Wyatt refuses to cooperate and withdraws. Leaving nothing behind for the looters, he sets fire to his wells, creating the spectacular and symbolic Wyatt's Torch.

Ragnar Danneskjold A notorious pirate and one of the first strikers. Danneskjold fights the looters on their own violent terms. A reverse Robin Hood, he steals from the parasites and returns wealth to the productive.

Dr. Robert Stadler Once a brilliant professor and scientist who taught physics to Galt, Danneskjold, and Francisco at Patrick Henry University, Stadler is the disillusioned head scientist at the State Science Institute. He allows the looters to appropriate his mind.

Hugh Akston A philosopher who champions reason, Akston taught Galt, Danneskjold, and Francisco at Patrick Henry University. He joins the strike early on, after society proclaims the death of reason. He works as a short-order cook in a diner.

Wesley Mouch Originally Rearden's "Washington Man," Mouch is a mediocre bureaucrat who rises to the role of economic dictator through his betrayal of Rearden and his well-placed connections.

Orren Boyle The corrupt owner of Associated Steel. Although his product is inferior to Rearden's, he uses his government connections to protect his business and obtain the rights to make Rearden Metal.

Cherryl Brooks A young, idealistic hero worshipper who marries Jim, mistakenly believing he is a good man. Jim seeks to destroy her and the good she represents, and is ultimately successful.

The Wet Nurse (Tony) A young bureaucrat sent by the government to watch over Rearden's mills. Though he starts out as a cynical follower of the looters' code, his experience at the mills transforms him, and he comes to respect and admire the producers.

Owen Kellogg A talented employee of Taggart and one of the first men in the novel to retire mysteriously.

Midas Mulligan The most successful banker of all time and the owner of the valley where the strikers live. Mulligan withdrew from society after realizing that he cannot thrive in a system that rewards need over ability.

Judge Narrangansett The legal mind that champions the freedom of individuals to produce and trade free of government intervention. He is one of the strikers who live in the valley.

Dr. Floyd Ferris The head of the State Science Institute and author of *Why Do You Think You Think?* Ferris rejects the mind and recognizes only bald power. He leads the faction that seeks to kill John Galt instead of working with him and jeopardizing its own power.

Mr. Thompson The Head of State, Thompson is pragmatic and driven only by the immediacy of the moment. He cynically believes that everyone, including Galt, is willing to cut a deal in exchange for power. He is genuinely stunned when Galt rejects his offer.

Richard Halley A brilliant composer who joins the strike after his work is praised only for having been borne of suffering. His fifth concerto is played throughout the strikers' valley.

Dan Conway The owner of the Phoenix-Durango Line in Colorado, who disappears after Taggart uses his influence to destroy his railroad with the Anti-dog-eat-dog Rule.

Ken Dannager A self-made Pennsylvania coal producer and friend of Rearden's. He recognizes the irrationality of the looters' laws and breaks them. He joins the strike after he is arrested for making illegal deals with Rearden.

Philip Rearden Hank Rearden's parasitic brother. He lives off of Rearden's accomplishments while simultaneously criticizing him for pursuing them.

ANALYSIS OF MAJOR CHARACTERS

JOHN GALT

Galt is the most important character in the novel and the driving force behind its action. The strike that he conceives, organizes, and carries out is the book's central, defining event. But his identity remains a mystery until two-thirds of the way through the novel, lending him a mythical stature. In Galt, Rand has set out to present man in his most ideal form. She describes him as physically beautiful, profoundly brilliant, and enormously accomplished. Not only has he been able to develop a revolutionary motor, he has also created a philosophy of reason and become a statesman capable of leading the world's most talented men. Most importantly, Galt is unwaveringly rational and deals directly with the objective facts he encounters. In him, rationality and emotion are fully integrated. Though ruled by reason, he is able to express and experience his emotions as well. Just as Rand uses Dagny to shatter the mind-body dichotomy that separates physical pleasure from higher thought, she employs Galt to reject the split between reason and emotion.

Galt represents the main theme of the novel and of Rand's philosophy: the idea that the mind is the only means by which man can achieve prosperity. The mind is the motive power that drives civilization, just as the motor Galt develops can drive industry. Galt embodies the mind, and the question "Who is John Galt?" is not only a literal question about the mysterious man who has disappeared, but a figurative question as well. The question asks *what is the mind?* and *what happens when the mind disappears?* Galt knows that without his mind and the minds of the world's great thinkers, the motive power of the world will be lost and the motor of the world will stop.

DAGNY TAGGART

Dagny is remarkable in every way: beautiful, talented, determined, and highly intelligent. Her independent spirit leads her to trust her own judgment over public opinion. Though calmly rational, she is also tremendously passionate about her work and love. She is enormously successful as a woman in a man's world. Rand presents her this way to demonstrate that rationality and great accomplishments are not gender-specific. Dagny's defining characteristic is a supreme self-confidence. She is keenly aware of her own abilities and always knows the right thing to do. But her confidence is also her flaw. She leaves the strikers and rejoins the real world because she feels she can single-handedly save her railroad and by extension her world. No one person can do this, and her realization comes nearly too late, as she is the last to join the strike. She is also flawed in her optimism about people. Until the end, when she learns the looters will torture Galt to make him help them, she continues to believe they can be made to understand their errors.

JAMES (JIM) TAGGART

Jim is the antithesis of the striking heroes in every aspect. Where they are brilliant, strong, and independent, he is weak and dependent on public opinion for every decision he makes. His only real skill is in influence peddling, and he uses it to improve Taggart's position in the industry and to destroy the great minds he envies and hates. Jim embodies Rand's concept of evil. His ambition in life is simply to destroy the good, making him a classic example of a nihilist. Because Jim's true nature is so terrible, he cannot bear to know it and spends a great deal of energy repressing it and convincing himself he is motivated by profit, public service, or love. He marries Cherryl Brooks in order to destroy her goodness but convinces himself he has done it for love. She is an easy target for him and a substitute for the great men like Rearden, whom he cannot manage to ruin. Eventually, Jim can no longer hide his nature from himself. Cherryl's suicide contributes to his awful realization. Finally, watching Galt's torture and screaming for him to die brings him face to face with his depravity. The realization causes him to go mad.

HANK REARDEN

Rearden is the embodiment of productivity, just as Galt represents the mind. His legendary capacity for hard work and his integrity and skill have made him the most successful industrialist in the country. At first, Rearden struggles with important misconceptions about himself that undermine his ability to see his own greatness.

He undergoes a profound transformation in the course of the novel. Despite operating his business based on a rational moral code that demands value for value, he allows his family to sponge off of him and make him feel guilty for his success. This makes him willing to sacrifice himself for their flawed morality and saps his vitality. He also mistakenly believes in a separation of the mind and body, which makes him see physical desire as base and low, and the things of the mind as unrelated to the physical world. Dagny and Francisco help him to reject this idea, which enables him to embrace his own value.

FRANCISCO D'ANCONIA

The wealthy and accomplished Francisco is a profoundly intelligent and highly successful man whose whole life is a paradox. He was the first man to join Galt's strike and serves as its recruiter, living in two worlds as he tries to bring others over to the strikers' side. Although he is a brilliant businessman, he deliberately destroys d'Anconia Copper and brings down the fortunes of many others with it. And although he has only ever loved Dagny, he plays the part of a promiscuous playboy as a cover for his real activities. He is enthusiastic and benevolent, although much of his strike-related activities cause others, especially Dagny and Rearden, to feel he is mocking and untrustworthy. Francisco has a profound effect on Rearden, whom he genuinely loves, even while knowing Rearden is Dagny's lover. He serves as Rearden's protector, arming him with the moral certainty he needs to battle the looters. He seems to appear at Rearden's side when he is needed most, and saves his life in the mill riots.

Francisco's commitment to the strike is absolute, but he suffers a great deal for it. First, he must give up Dagny and allow her to view him as depraved and worthless. Later, he must endure Rearden's hatred as well, when he is forced to betray him in a copper deal. And he must continually work to destroy the company his family built for generations. But the suffering is worth the price for him, because he is sure that he is right. Eventually, Dagny and Rearden come to understand and admire him, and the strike he devotes his life to works as planned.

THEMES, MOTIFS & SYMBOLS

THEMES

Themes are the fundamental and often universal ideas explored in a literary work.

THE IMPORTANCE OF THE MIND
The "strike of the mind" led by John Galt demonstrates this central theme of the novel. When the best creative minds are systematically removed from the world, their importance is laid bare. Without the great thinkers, society spirals quickly downward. The economy collapses, and irrational looters seize power. Rand's belief in the central importance of the mind opposes the prevailing wisdom that labor is responsible for prosperity. As the events of the novel show, the mind enables creation and innovation and powers the engine of the world. Labor alone cannot achieve productivity and prosperity without the guidance of the mind.

THE EVILS OF COLLECTIVISM
Rand sets out to demonstrate through the novel's action what happens when governments follow socialist ideas. She argues that when men are compelled, through collectivism's forced moral code, to place the needs of their neighbors above their own rational self-interest, the result is chaos and evil. Incentive is destroyed, and corruption becomes inevitable. The story of the Twentieth Century Motor Company illustrates this brilliantly. After the plant adopted a method in which workers were paid according to perceived needs and ordered to work based on perceived ability, the workers became depraved and immoral, each seeking to show himself or herself as most needy and least skilled. The plant failed, and the community was destroyed by mistrust and greed. For Rand, any economic or political plan based on sacrifice of the individual for the group leads to chaos and destruction.

THE NEED TO INTEGRATE MIND AND BODY

Rand rejects the mind-body dichotomy that is central to many philosophies and religions. She opposes the idea that the thoughts and achievements of the mind are pure and noble, but the desires of the body are base and immoral, and she presents Dagny as a character who also rejects the idea. Dagny is proud of her sexuality and sees her physical desires flowing logically from the evaluations and rationality of her mind. At first, Rearden accepts the mind-body split. His transformation occurs when he comes to integrate the two facets of himself into a rational whole.

Dr. Stadler represents another aspect of this mind-body dichotomy. He sees the pure science of the mind as removed from practical affairs and wonders why the mind that made the motor would bother with practical applications. For him, the mind is cut off not just from the body but from practical life. Again, Dagny represents the integrated whole when she concludes that the motor's inventor worked within the reality of practical life because he liked living on earth.

MOTIFS

Motifs are recurring structures, contrasts, or literary devices that can help to develop and inform the text's major themes.

RHETORICAL QUESTIONS

The literary device of rhetorical questioning frequently draws attention to key thematic elements. The most obvious example is the unanswerable "Who is John Galt?" The question takes on many layers of meaning: as a slang reference to hopelessness and futility, as a source for speculation about the mythical figure who may have found Atlantis, and finally as a public response to Galt's radio broadcast. Stadler's "What can you do when you have to deal with people?" is another recurring rhetorical question that takes on different meaning based on context. For example, Stadler's disillusioned question is turned against him when Floyd Ferris uses it to coerce him into speaking at the demonstration of Project X.

MOTIVE POWER

Motors are everywhere in the novel. The revolutionary motor built by John Galt embodies the power to harness energy and move things with it. Metaphorically, the motive power of the world is in the rational mind, and when the mind is withdrawn, the "motor of the world" begins to stop. In a real sense, motive power is essential to Dagny, who continually searches for decent locomotives to pull her trains.

BRIDGES

Bridges serve to represent the great things that can be accomplished by the application of the mind. Rearden's design for the bridge on the John Galt Line, the first to be made from Rearden Metal, shows a creative solution to a problem that he takes joy in solving. Similarly, the great Taggart Bridge, which links the East and West in a single transcontinental line, represents the product of Dagny's grandfather Nathaniel's tireless effort and ingenuity. The destruction of the bridge in the Project X disaster demonstrates that the products of the creative mind are no longer appreciated or understood, and the end is near.

SYMBOLS

Symbols are objects, characters, figures, or colors used to represent abstract ideas or concepts.

THE SIGN OF THE DOLLAR

The dollar sign is the symbol of the strikers. Their cigarettes are stamped with it, and their town square displays a giant dollar sign. For them, the symbol is not merely shorthand for money, but a symbol of a way of life. The dollar sign represents the things it is exchanged for, namely, the productive abilities of man and the goods and services created by the mind at work. The very existence of money suggests that there are goods produced and people able to produce them, which is what makes money meaningful and valued. In his "money speech," Francisco says, "To trade by means of money is the code of the men of good will." The strikers value the dollar so much that they have their own mint in the valley and use only gold as the standard for exchange.

THE BRACELET

The bracelet Rearden creates from the first batch of Rearden Metal symbolizes everything he has worked toward for ten years, and in a larger sense, the purest product of the unfettered, creative mind. It represents his pride in and love for his work, and he wants desperately to share these values with someone. Lillian, who hates and wants to destroy Rearden, misses the point entirely and wears the bracelet only to mock him. She wrongly interprets its meaning as a reference to her bondage, though it is clearly Rearden who is chained to her. Dagny, on the other hand, understands all that the bracelet stands for and shares the values it represents, as demonstrated by her insistence on trading her diamonds for it. In their reactions to the bracelet, we see a sharp contrast between the two women, and it becomes clear that Dagny is the one for Rearden.

WYATT'S TORCH

Before Ellis Wyatt disappears to join the strike, he destroys his own oil fields by setting fire to them, and the fires continue to burn night and day. Wyatt's Torch, as the huge flame comes to be known, symbolizes his unwillingness to sanction and participate in the looters' system or to offer them any useful resources to drain. The flame is a powerful symbol of individualism and the refusal to surrender the mind. Wyatt's Torch is the very last thing the passengers see before dying in the Taggart Tunnel disaster and the only part of the outside world visible to the residents of the valley.

ATLAS

Atlas, the hero of Greek mythology who carried the weight of the heavens on his shoulders, symbolizes the exploited industrialists, particularly Rearden, whose hard work and great strength support the parasites who live off their productive capabilities. When Francisco tells Rearden that he would advise Atlas to shrug and let go of his burden, he is referring to the strike and calling upon Rearden to lay down his burden and stop believing it is his duty to bear so much weight for the undeserving. Rearden's only reward for his efforts is the persecution of a corrupt government and the exhaustion of carrying others. Francisco knows it is unjust for Rearden, or anyone, to be cast in this role. By recruiting him for the strike, he tries to show Rearden a way out.

Summary & Analysis

Part One, Chapters I–II

Summary—Chapter I: The Theme

Eddie Willers, special assistant to the vice president of Taggart Transcontinental, walks toward his New York office. An anonymous homeless man asks, "Who is John Galt?" after Eddie gives him some money. Eddie is disturbed by the phrase, a slang reference to all that is hopeless and unknowable. As he looks around, he sees businesses failing everywhere. He remembers an oak tree he saw destroyed by lightning as a child. Eddie meets with the railroad's president, James (Jim) Taggart, about another wreck on the Rio Norte Line. He argues that the track must be replaced, but Taggart says he cannot do anything until the new track arrives from Orren Boyle's Associated Steel. Eddie wants to use Rearden Steel, but Jim reminds him that Boyle is a good friend and deserves a break. Eddie counters that they risk losing every major shipper in Colorado to the Phoenix-Durango, a rapidly growing young railroad run by Dan Conway. They have already lost the support of Ellis Wyatt, an entrepreneur who has found a way to revive exhausted oil wells. Wyatt Oil switched to the Phoenix-Durango when Taggart could not keep up with its shipments. Jim tells Eddie that nothing can be done.

After a trip to examine the Rio Norte Line, Dagny Taggart, Eddie's boss and Jim's sister, sits aboard a train, listening to the notes of a fantastic symphony. It turns out to be just a brakeman whistling. He tells her the tune is Richard Halley's Fifth Concerto. When she tells him that is impossible, since Halley only wrote four concertos, he becomes evasive. Later, Dagny awakes to find the train has stopped. When she investigates, she finds the engineer refuses to take responsibility for moving the train ahead. She identifies herself and orders him to move the train. Seeing how hard it is to find good men, she makes a note to herself to promote a talented employee named Owen Kellogg.

At a meeting with her brother Jim, Dagny tells him that the problems with the Rio Norte are worse than they thought, so she has canceled the order with Orren Boyle and placed an order with Rearden Steel for a new alloy called Rearden Metal. Jim complains that she had no authority from the Board and that they should give Boyle a chance as a "little guy" up against the larger Rearden Steel. He denounces her choice of Rearden Metal, an unproven new material that no one has been willing to try. Dagny does not care what the others are doing. She knows that Rearden Metal is the best substance on the market. Jim evades the issue, but finally agrees to put the order through.

Dagny calls the Music Publishing Company to inquire about Halley's Fifth Concerto, but is told that Halley has dropped out of public life and has not published anything in eight years. Owen Kellogg comes to see Dagny. Before she can offer him a promotion, he informs her that he is quitting. She tries to discover his reason, but he seems to have none. She offers him anything he wants to stay, but he refuses. If he loves his job, she asks, why leave? He shrugs and answers, "Who is John Galt?"

SUMMARY—CHAPTER II: THE CHAIN

Hank Rearden watches happily as the first heat for the first order of Rearden Metal is poured. As he walks home, he thinks of the ten years of trial and effort that yielded the new alloy and of his early years of hard work in the mines and his steady rise to ownership of mines and mills. Arriving home he finds his wife talking to his mother, his brother Philip, and Paul Larkin, an unsuccessful businessman and old friend. He apologizes for being late but finds that he cannot tell them about Rearden Metal, knowing they will not share his joy. His family insults him and his devotion to his work, scolding him for working so much and not caring about them. He presents his wife Lillian with a bracelet, a chain poured from the first order of Rearden Metal. His mother reprimands him for thinking that his metal should be like diamonds to his wife. Rearden feels only an incredible sense of exhaustion and confusion over what his family wants from him. Although he supports them, they seem to want to hold some claim over him. They profess love for him, but despise all the qualities in him that he feels are worthy of love. Paul Larkin approaches Rearden and advises him to ease up on his individualism. He reminds Rearden that he should pay attention to "his man in Washington." Rearden knows that every day it becomes more important to have a strong lobbyist and protection against the legislature, but he cannot bring himself to think about it with any conviction.

ANALYSIS: PART ONE, CHAPTERS I–II

In these early chapters, Rand clearly establishes the state of the nation. Decay is rampant and unavoidable. Businesses are failing, and companies that remain in business face shortages and delays. People respond with a helpless sense of doom, epitomized in the rhetorical question, "Who is John Galt?" The question represents a melancholy shrug, a declaration of defenselessness before a force too terrifying and massive to combat or even comprehend—a pervasive hopelessness and loss of spirit. The oak tree that Eddie remembers serves as an apt metaphor for society's decay. Eddie recalls that after lightning struck the tree, he looked inside to see that it was already dead, and the trunk had been a mere shell all along. Similarly, society has begun to decay from the inside out.

From our first introduction to them, we see the sharp contrast between Dagny and her brother Jim. Each represents a different side in the central struggle of the book. Dagny is strong, bold, and confident, and represents Rand's vision of capitalism. She finds joy in productive, meaningful work. She makes decisions based on rational, objective facts. Her choice of Rearden Metal is based solely on her study of its merits and potential to yield profit. Jim, on the other hand, is weak and depends on public opinion for his decisions. He fears using Rearden Metal simply because no one else has used it yet. He is an example of Rand's view of socialism, with its focus on sacrificing for the public good and helping "little guys" even when others have better products.

The issues of personal responsibility and commitment to work are also demonstrated in these chapters. The weak deflect blame and refuse to take actions for which they might be held responsible, while the strong rely on their own judgment and accept responsibility. The engineer on the train will not move it from its siding until Dagny agrees to be responsible for the orders. Jim argues that the situation on the Rio Norte Line is not his fault and refuses to agree to the purchase of Rearden Metal unless Dagny will take responsibility for it. In this environment of deflection and apathy, men of talent appear to be disappearing, a fact that Dagny has begun to notice. The withdrawal of Richard Halley from public life is mysterious, even more so after Dagny hears his Fifth Concerto (which does not exist, according to his publishing company) whistled by a brakeman on the train. She is also perplexed by the retirement of Owen Kellogg. Despite a promising career at Taggart, he leaves a job he loves, offering no reason and no stated plans. Dagny wonders why the irresponsible remain while the talented men seem to be first to quit.

In Hank Rearden, Rand offers an example of a successful industrialist moved to joy by the fruits of his own labor. He believes in what he can see and make, and is driven above all else by his love for his work. He is self-motivated and self-actualized, though his family calls him selfish. He is selfish in the sense that he is motivated to do things for himself, not for the benefit of others. For Ayn Rand, being motivated by his own values makes Rearden not only successful but virtuous. His family stands in sharp contrast to him. They are driven by their own weakness to take from him, while encouraging him to feel guilty. Their ability to control him depends on his acceptance of his guilt. This dynamic is central to the looters' way of life. By making the strong feel guilty for their strength and responsible for the weak, the looters are able to continue living off producers without producing anything themselves. Rearden fails to understand this paradigm in his personal life even while recognizing it in his work. This split in his personality represents a weakness he must overcome. When he gives the bracelet of Rearden Metal to Lillian, she comments that it represents the bondage in which he keeps them, but clearly Rearden is the one enslaved to his family.

The seemingly casual conversation between Rearden and Paul Larkin offers the reader an ominous foreshadowing of the political events to come. As a self-made man, Rearden has little patience for the games one must play in politics. Preferring to spend his time in his lab and mills, he has not been closely involved in his "Washington Man's" activities, an omission that will have grave consequences.

PART ONE, CHAPTERS III–IV

SUMMARY—CHAPTER III: THE TOP AND THE BOTTOM

In a dark bar, four men discuss the state of the nation's economy. Orren Boyle argues that Rearden Steel has an unfair advantage because it owns iron mines, while his Associated Steel does not. Jim Taggart agrees to use his influence in Washington to force Rearden to give up the mines. Paul Larkin, also at the meeting, agrees to receive the mines from Rearden but give the ore directly to Boyle. In return, Jim wants Boyle to convince friends on the National Alliance of Railroads to force Dan Conway out of Colorado on the grounds that his Phoenix-Durango Line offers "cutthroat competition" to

Taggart in a state where Taggart had operations first. Wesley Mouch, Rearden's Washington Man, is also present. In return for Mouch's not warning Rearden, Jim agrees to find him a bureaucratic post in Washington. Their conversation shifts to Mexico, where Jim has built the San Sebastian Line. There are rumors that Mexico is going to nationalize the line, but Boyle refutes them. He tells Jim that on a recent visit, he rode in old, run-down trains.

Back at the office, Jim confronts Dagny about the shoddy trains. She tells him she has removed everything of value from the San Sebastian Line to minimize Taggart's losses if Mexico nationalizes the line. They argue about the San Sebastian Line, the first major project Jim began after becoming president of Taggart, and one Dagny has opposed from the beginning, believing the resources were needed on the Rio Norte Line. Jim reminds her that Mexico has guaranteed their property rights for two hundred years and argues that he built it for the good of the Mexican people. But he also built the line in order to reap a huge profit from the nearby d'Anconia copper mines. Dagny reminds him that Francisco d'Anconia, formerly an industrial genius, has become a worthless playboy in recent years and has yet to produce any copper from the mines.

Eddie Willers enters the cafeteria of the Taggart Terminal. He sits, as he often does, with a grease-stained worker. Eddie has always liked this worker and feels comfortable with him, although he does not know his name. Eddie complains about the decay slowly eating the world and the railroad. He has hope, however, because Dagny has found a reliable contractor and is going to fix the Rio Norte Line. The worker inquires about Dagny's personal life, and Eddie tells him what he knows. He is surprised by the worker's interest.

SUMMARY — CHAPTER IV: THE IMMOVABLE MOVERS
Eddie informs Dagny that McNamara, their new contractor, has just quit, offering no reasons. No one knows where he has gone. The People's State of Mexico nationalizes the San Sebastian Railroad and the d'Anconia copper mines. In his report to the Board of Directors, Jim takes full credit for Dagny's decision to remove the most valuable equipment from Mexico before the San Sebastian Railroad was nationalized.

The members of the National Alliance of Railroads approve a proposal known as the "Anti-dog-eat-dog Rule," designed to reduce competition among railroads. According to the proposal, the interests of the whole industry are to be determined by majority vote, and each company must subordinate itself to the majority's decision. Dagny goes to see Dan Conway, president of the Phoenix-Durango railroad, which will cease to exist under the new rule. She urges him to fight, but he is too tired and has decided to retire. Dagny had intended to compete with him in Colorado, but she cannot stand to defeat him in this fashion. She feels like a looter. He tells her to get her Rio Norte Line up and running quickly, because the fate of Ellis Wyatt depends on it. Ellis Wyatt comes to see Dagny and tells her angrily that she must fix the Rio Norte Line at once. He issues her an ultimatum. If she does not give him the transportation he needs, he will take her company down with him. She tells him that he will have the transportation he needs in time. He is surprised, having expected excuses and evasion.

Dagny goes to see Hank Rearden. She tells him about the Wyatt meeting and tells him they must rebuild the line in nine months, not twelve. He assures her that he will be able to provide what she needs. Rearden is surprised and delighted that she deals with him on his own level and thinks he has finally met a woman he can understand. He tells her that it is people like them who move the world and who will ultimately pull it through.

ANALYSIS: PART ONE, CHAPTERS III–IV

In the decaying world, business is now done in backroom bars and involves manipulation and deceit. Instead of trading value for value, the looters trade favors. Influence has become a form of currency and a basis for decisions that defy logic. As a result, the weak profit at the expense of the strong. Taggart lost business to Conway's Phoenix-Durango Line because Conway offered a better service, but Conway will lose anyway because of the involvement of influence peddlers. Similarly, Boyle will profit at the expense of Rearden, although Rearden's product is far superior. Although the overall harm to the industries seems minimal now, this trend, if left unchecked, may have grave consequences. In sharp contrast, Dagny, Rearden, and Wyatt engage in straightforward and honest dealings. For these industrialists, business transactions depend solely on mutual self-interest. They buy the best goods at the best prices and sell their best products for the highest price they can get. Wyatt's shock at the straight answers he receives from Dagny when he confronts her about fixing the Rio Norte Line demonstrate how rare this candor has become in an era of evasion and double-speak.

Jim's actions reveal the corruption behind the so-called altruism of socialist endeavors. He argues publicly that he has built the San Sebastian Line to bring service to the Mexican people, who have no railroads of their own. In fact, he is motivated by the profits he hopes to make from the d'Anconia mines as well as by the desire to improve his stature among his Washington friends by helping the government appear self-sacrificing in regard to the poor Mexicans. Throughout the novel, laws and directives presented by the government as protection for a fragile economy contain similar hidden motives. Behind them all are looters who stand, not coincidentally, to gain in profit and influence.

Rand's warnings about the effects of socialism begin to build. The book's characters still regard the nationalization of the San Sebastian Line, along with the creation of "People's States" all over the world as a faraway event. For most readers, Communism is a similarly remote threat. But Rand had firsthand experience with the effects of nationalization and the creation of a Communist state, and her hatred of the system is more than just ideological. Throughout the novel, threats become more and more immediate. Rights are gradually eroded, and individuals give themselves up to the group until the government gains control of everything and destroys society in the process. The passage of the Anti-dog-eat-dog Rule illustrates the mistakes that occur when individuals submit to majority rule. Dan Conway knows the rule is wrong, morally and economically, but he feels he has no choice but to abide by the majority's decision. In effect, he surrenders his mind to the group and allows himself to support the destruction of his own business. For Rand, nothing could be worse than the idea that a rational man must subordinate himself to an irrational group.

Some important mysteries are introduced in these chapters. We learn that Francisco has been one of the most successful businessmen of all time. His endeavors are so successful that Jim willingly risks millions of dollars on his unproved mines. When Dagny points out that Francisco is no longer the man he was, having degenerated from unlimited potential to a playboy's life of decadence, we learn that she has known him well in the past. The questions raised for the reader are: Why would such a man choose to squander his talents? Why do so many talented men like him continue to disappear? Where do they go? Why do they seem to vanish just when they are needed most, as did McNamara the contractor? Who is the man Eddie dines with in the cafeteria, and why is he so interested in Dagny?

PART ONE, CHAPTERS V–VI

SUMMARY — CHAPTER V: THE CLIMAX OF THE D'ANCONIAS

The Mexican government has discovered, upon nationalizing Francisco d'Anconia's San Sebastian mines, that the mines are completely worthless. Dagny is furious. On her way to confront Francisco, she remembers the way he used to be. His summer visits were the highlight of her childhood, as they played together and dreamed of taking over their families' businesses. Later, they had become lovers. But the affair ended ten years ago when Francisco left her. Leaving was torture for him, but he said he had no choice and warned her not to ask any questions. He said that he would do things that soon would make her denounce him, and she has. Over the next few years, Francisco became the most notorious playboy in the world, squandering his fortune on foolishness.

Dagny confronts Francisco. She asks him why he deliberately invested in worthless mines and ruined the fortunes of his stockholders, among them James Taggart. She tells him that he should be fighting hardest against the looters of the world. He responds that in fact he is fighting against her and her railroad. She is horrified. She asks him what he is trying to do, and why, but he tells her that she is not ready to hear it. She does not have enough courage yet.

SUMMARY — CHAPTER VI: THE NON-COMMERCIAL

Lillian Rearden throws a party to celebrate her wedding anniversary. Hank Rearden agrees to attend out of a sense of duty, though he dreads it. He would rather be working to find a replacement for the recently resigned superintendent of one of his mills. Dagny also attends. Although she feels there is much to celebrate in the progress of the Colorado track, Rearden is unexpectedly cold toward her.

The party guests are writers, intellectuals, and other important figures in society. Their conversations suggest the futility of the times. Dr. Pritchett argues that man is nothing but a collection of chemicals, with only instinct as his guide. Ralph Eubank contends that true literature is about suffering and defeat, because it is impossible to be happy. The only thing one can live for is "brother-love." The intellectuals agree that need is the only valid consideration, that whatever is good for society is right.

Francisco d'Anconia enters the party. Rearden asks Lillian to keep Francisco away from him. Jim Taggart pulls d'Anconia aside to confront him about the San Sebastian mines. Francisco responds that he only did what the entire world is now preaching. He hired men not because they were competent, but because they needed the work. He did not work for profit, but took a loss. Everyone criticizes industrialists for their domineering nature, so he simply let his underlings control the venture. Jim is helpless and furious.

After some time, Francisco approaches Rearden and tells him that he came to the party simply because he wanted to meet him. He approaches him with such sincerity that Rearden finds himself listening. Francisco's message is mysterious, but Rearden is drawn to it. He asks why Rearden carries so many people, why he is willing to work and let others feed off his energy. Rearden responds that it is because they are weak and that he does not mind the burden. Francisco corrects him and tells him the others are not weak; they have his own guilt as a weapon against him. A woman at the party professes to know the identity of John Galt. She says Galt was a millionaire who discovered Atlantis. Dagny does not believe the story, but Francisco steps in and announces that he does.

Dagny admires Lillian's bracelet made of Rearden Metal. When Lillian mockingly complains that she would gladly exchange it for diamonds, Dagny offers her own diamond bracelet, which Lillian is forced to accept. Rearden watches, visibly shaken, but stands by his wife, coldly telling Dagny that her action was not necessary.

ANALYSIS: PART ONE, CHAPTERS V–VI

The mystery of Francisco deepens as readers learn what he has done. By deliberately investing in worthless mines, he has destroyed his own fortune. What could possibly have motivated him? Dagny's memory of their affair reveals him to be even more complicated. Clearly, he loved her very much, yet he chose to leave her and pursue a worthless existence, seemingly against his own desires. The question of why he left her and why he is working to destroy her railroad along with his mines is at the heart of the novel. But neither Dagny nor the reader is ready to know the answers just yet.

Lillian's party guests demonstrate the cynical and hopeless state of the culture. Intellectuals speak aimlessly of the futility of thought, the death of reason, and the supremacy of need. When Francisco tells Jim his mismanagement of the mines was merely putting society's vague words into action, he begins to demonstrate the absurdity involved in the practical application of socialist ideas. But Jim does not hear him or understand the absurdity. He is too focused on his own losses. Francisco has put the conventional morality into action, with disastrous effect. His comments foreshadow the absurdity to come, as lawmakers create policies that are contradictory and illogical, then wonder at their failure.

The party also serves to bring Francisco and Rearden together. The dignity Francisco shows in approaching Rearden disarms him and makes him open to the strange message Francisco bears. Francisco's respectful tone is even more surprising and unexpected, given his playboy reputation. This conversation marks the beginning of Rearden's transformation as he struggles to overcome his dual nature. As Francisco points out, Rearden is an uncompromising egoist who happily follows his own rational self-interest in his work. But in his personal life, he allows others to dictate his morality and accepts condemnation from a family that leeches off of him, offering him no value in exchange. When Francisco points out this duality, Rearden begins to close the gap between his two selves. But he still does not understand why Francisco has told him all this.

Rand uses the bracelet incident to create important contrasts between Dagny and Lillian. Dagny's love for the bracelet demonstrates that she understands what is important to Rearden and that the same things are important to her. Lillian, on the other hand, hates the bracelet and wears it only to mock Rearden. She does not understand or care for him at all. Although he despises Lillian, Rearden is trapped in an imposed morality and feels compelled to stand by his wife. He assumes that his inability to understand her must be a failure within himself. Although Rearden understands how much he and Dagny have in common and is attracted to her, he treats her coldly in an attempt to resist the attraction and remain loyal to his mocking wife.

The mystery of John Galt continues to grow as the guests discuss the rumor that he discovered the legendary Atlantis, a paradise on Earth. Francisco's insistence that the story is true creates a possible link between his own mysterious secrets and the answer to the question "Who is John Galt?"

Part One, Chapters VII–VIII

Summary — Chapter VII: The Exploiters and the Exploited

> *But what can you do when you have to deal with people?*
>
> *(See* Quotations, *p. 66)*

The reconstruction of the Rio Norte Line is plagued with problems, but Dagny and Rearden manage to keep the project on schedule through quick and decisive actions. Ellis Wyatt appears at the Rio Norte construction site, where he has been helping out behind the scenes. His appreciative tone with Dagny acknowledges that she is as driven and focused as he is. Dagny is relieved to also find Rearden at the site. He proposes replacing an old bridge in Colorado with one made entirely of Rearden Metal. Dagny approves his bold plan.

Back in New York, Dagny orders a cup of coffee at a diner. A man sitting next to her complains that there is no human spirit, that men are concerned only with satisfying their bodies' needs. Another man shrugs off the importance of morality. "Who is John Galt?" he says with a sneer. At this, a small, shriveled tramp declares that he knows. John Galt was a great explorer who found the fountain of youth.

Dr. Potter, from the State Science Institute, comes to see Rearden and tells him that society is not ready for Rearden Metal. He says that Rearden's company might harm his competitors by producing too much and asks Rearden to wait a few years before producing his metal. When Rearden refuses, Potter offers to buy all rights to his metal, at any price. Rearden refuses. Potter tells him that there are certain bills pending in the legislature that make businessmen particularly vulnerable. The threat is clear. Later, the State Science Institute issues a formal warning about Rearden Metal. The statement lacks any scientific basis but hints at possible dangers. In response to the denunciation, Taggart stock crashes; Ben Nealy, the Taggart contractor, quits; the Brotherhood of Road and Track Workers forbids its members to work with the metal; and Jim leaves town.

Visiting the State Science Institute in New Hampshire, Dagny finds that Dr. Stadler, at one time the greatest scientist in the country, is completely disillusioned. He agrees that the metal is a great discovery but says the Institute will not support it. Despite spending millions, the Institute's metallurgists have failed to discover anything as valuable, and they are afraid to draw attention to the fact that a private citizen succeeded where a government-funded institution failed.

When Dagny finds Jim, he is desperate. He wants to save the railroad but has no idea what to do. Dagny tells him she will finish the line on her own. Because everyone is afraid of Rearden Metal, she will resign and start her own company. After she proves that the metal works, she will return to Taggart and bring her line with her. She will name her company the John Galt Line. Dagny goes to Francisco d'Anconia for money, but he refuses to help and expresses shock at her name for the line. Dagny finds the investors she needs among the industrialists of Colorado. Rearden also invests.

The Legislature passes the Equalization of Opportunity Bill, which will force Rearden to give up his mines. Wesley Mouch had not informed Rearden that the bill was being considered, and he cannot be reached by phone.

> Contradictions do not exist. Whenever you think that
> you are facing a contradiction, check your premises.
> You will find that one of them is wrong.
> (See QUOTATIONS, p. 67)

SUMMARY—CHAPTER VIII: THE JOHN GALT LINE

Rearden sells his ore mines to Paul Larkin and his coal mines to Ken Dannager, a self-made businessman from Pennsylvania. With the money from these sales, Rearden offers Taggart a moratorium on its debt to Rearden Steel. He knows that Taggart is having financial problems, and he wants the company to survive long enough to be his long-term customers. Rearden still cannot reach Wesley Mouch. He reads in the papers that Mouch has been appointed assistant coordinator of the Bureau of Economic Planning and National Resources.

As the date of the line's opening approaches, public criticism grows steadily louder. But when Dagny asks for volunteers to run the first train, every engineer at the company offers. Dagny holds a press conference in her office in which she proudly states that she expects to make a huge profit, and many are amazed at her admitted self-interest. Dagny and Rearden ride together in the engine of the first locomotive to ride the John Galt Line. The first run is a resounding success, spreading a mood of optimism and possibility among those who witness it. People line up all along the route, thrilled to finally have something to celebrate. Despite dire predictions, the bridge made of Rearden Metal holds up well. That night, at Ellis Wyatt's house, Dagny and Rearden make love for the first time.

ANALYSIS: PART ONE, CHAPTERS VII–VIII

Rand's heroes are bold and decisive, just as their enemies are soft and wavering. Acting with clarity and self-assurance, Dagny and Rearden expertly handle the rebuilding of the Rio Norte Line, even in the face of dramatic setbacks. They rely on facts alone to make decisions. Dagny agrees to build a bridge made of Rearden Metal because she knows the the metal's value will speak for itself. In contrast, Jim is paralyzed by public opinion. He has no rational judgment of his own but assumes that if "everyone" thinks something, they must be right. When Dagny boldly decides to build her own line as the only way to get it done, she demonstrates the creative power of the individual against the destructive power of the state. She knows she is right, and this is all the validation she requires. The second John Galt story shows him to be bold and heroic as well. Here he is credited with finding the fountain of youth. But what makes a person young and vital or old and wasted? In Rand's work, the physical descriptions of characters offer some clues. The industrialists, who use their minds as motive power and find joy in producing, are described as young, attractive, and vital, while the looters and moochers are dour, sullen, and formless. The fountain of youth in this context refers to the vitality of producing.

Rand demonstrates her belief that socialism destroys innovation by having the State Science Institute denounce Rearden Metal. When the state controls scientific development, it will be hesitant to allow private discoveries to come to light if they are seen as competition. State control of research and development not only slows the pace of innovation, but throws open the possibility of corruption and misuse of resources to further the political power of the state. Dr. Stadler embodies the disillusionment that results when the scientific mind is given over to the state. As a scientist, he should be devoted to the truth, but his priority has become political expediency. Although he knows that the State Science Institute's smear campaign against Rearden Metal is fabricated, he will do nothing about it for fear of risking his clout and the government funding on which he depends. In one of the classic paradoxes of socialism, a great scientific mind becomes employed in hindering the progress of science.

In Rand's view, when the government controls the economy, corruption and mediocrity are inevitable. Since the state has the power to grant economic favors, it naturally attracts those who seek to profit from them. People who cannot succeed in open competition find ways to rise once competitive barriers are artificially removed. Wesley Mouch is a significant character only in the sense that he is insignificant, a nobody able to rise through favors and manipulation instead of skill and hard work. In contrast, the success of the new John Galt Line is the triumph of hard work over mediocrity and of individual ambition over government barriers. Dagny and Rearden's first sexual encounter is also a manifestation of triumph. Their shared values and commitment to quality and truth have made the John Galt Line possible. Their joy is made physical in a natural, inevitable way.

PART ONE, CHAPTERS IX–X

SUMMARY — CHAPTER IX: THE SACRED AND THE PROFANE
After a night of passionate lovemaking, Dagny and Rearden wake together. Rearden is angry and disgusted. He sees sex as a base and obscene impulse and believes both Dagny and he worthy of contempt. Dagny laughs in disagreement. She is proud to make love to him and share her desire with someone she respects. She tells him she makes no claims on him except that he come to her with his lowest physical desires.

Jim meets Cherryl Brooks, a young, poor shopgirl who recognizes him from the newspapers. She thinks he is responsible for the success of the John Galt Line, and he allows her to believe it. Cherryl worships heroes and their accomplishments, and Jim enjoys the attention. He invites her to his apartment for a drink. She finds some of his comments odd, especially his contempt for Hank Rearden, whom she believes is a great man, but she is thrilled to be with him.

Dagny and Rearden go away for a vacation together, driving around the countryside. Hoping to locate some scarce machine tools, they stop at the site of the Twentieth Century Motor Company manufacturing plant. They are shocked to find the plant not just closed, but ruined, and the town it supported in abject poverty. Inside the plant's lab they find the remnants of a motor designed to run on static electricity. Its existence would revolutionize industrial production. They are determined to find the inventor and rebuild it.

Summary—Chapter X: Wyatt's Torch

Wesley Mouch, recently promoted to top coordinator of the Bureau of Economic Planning and National Resources, issues a number of statements urging the use of emergency powers to balance the economy. The Union of Locomotive Engineers demands that the maximum speed of all trains be reduced to sixty miles an hour. The Union of Railway Conductors and Brakemen demands that the length of all freight trains be reduced to sixty cars. The states of Wyoming, New Mexico, Utah, and Arizona demand that the number of trains run in Colorado not exceed the number running in each of these neighboring states. A group headed by Orren Boyle demands the passage of a law limiting the production of Rearden Metal to an amount equal to the output of any other steel mill of equal capacity. Another group demands a law giving every customer who wants it an equal supply of Rearden Metal. Still another group seeks to prevent eastern businesses from moving out of state, hoping to stop the trend of businesses relocating to Colorado. Rearden finds that Paul Larkin did not deliver his supply of ore. He sent it to Orren Boyle instead (as a term of the deal arranged earlier by Jim Taggart). After this, Rearden begins to obtain ore through shady illegal deals, the only option left to him.

Dagny's search for the motor's inventor leads her to Lee Hunsacker. He tells her that he purchased the factory from the heirs of Jed Starnes. He had asked Midas Mulligan, the richest man in the country, for a loan, but Mulligan had refused him. When Mulligan refused, Hunsacker filed suit against him. The judge in charge, Judge Narragansett, ruled for Mulligan, but Hunsacker appealed. A higher court ordered Mulligan to issue the loan based solely on Hunsacker's "need" and despite his lack of ability or collateral. Instead of paying, Mulligan disappeared without a trace. Narragansett disappeared a few months later. When Dagny locates Starnes's heirs, she discovers why the company fell apart. It had been run according to a radical plan in which workers were paid based only on their proclaimed needs, and those who worked hardest were required to support those who did not. The resulting chaos destroyed the company. Dagny finds the wife of William Hastings, the former chief engineer. She sends Dagny to find a man who she thinks would know the name of the inventor. Dagny finds him working as a cook in a Wyoming diner. He does know the inventor, but he will not give the name. Dagny is shocked to learn the cook is

Hugh Akston, a famous philosopher who retired years ago. He gives her a mysterious cigarette stamped with the sign of the dollar.

When Dagny returns to New York, she finds that every law the looters were seeking has been passed. A special tax has been imposed on the state of Colorado. Dagny tries to reach the defiant Ellis Wyatt, but when she gets to Colorado, she sees that he has set fire to his oil fields and disappeared.

ANALYSIS: PART ONE, CHAPTERS IX–X

Dagny's rejection of Rearden's critical view of sex reflects Rand's attitude that the mind and body cannot be separated. Rearden sees the achievements of the mind as noble but the desires of the body as base and unrelated to the mind. In contrast, Dagny (like Rand) sees the desires of the body stemming naturally from the rational mind. Dagny desires Rearden precisely because her mind perceives the value of his great accomplishments, and she knows he chooses her for the same reasons. Therefore, she sees sex as a grand expression of the values they represent to each other, not as a shameful impulse. Rearden must learn to integrate the mind and body if he is to be released from his self-made bonds.

Jim and Cherryl's romance is entirely different. Cherryl chooses Jim because of the values she thinks he represents, but she is wrong about him. Jim chooses Cherryl out of his need to destroy. Although he claims to have noble, altruistic goals and a desire to help the "little guy," his true nature is to destroy the efforts and aspirations of others. The young hero-worshipper is easy prey, much easier to destroy than Dagny, Rearden, or Francisco. However, neither Jim nor Cherryl are aware of his nature—yet.

When she discovers the remnants of the motor, Dagny has a new motivating purpose in the story. With its potential to revolutionize not only the transportation industry, but every industry, Dagny knows the motor could save a crumbling society. Finding its inventor and rebuilding it gradually become even more important than saving her railroad. Also, the motor represents the concept of motive power. It can power a society, just as a locomotive engine can power a train. In Ayn Rand's philosophy, the mind, fueled by rational thought, is the motive power that fuels man's existence.

The new laws demonstrate the absurdity of socialism in action. There is no way the businesses affected by them can possibly survive in the long term if they are to follow the rules. For example, if Taggart must run fewer, shorter, and slower trains through Colorado, it will lose money through increased operating costs and lower shipping fees. Meanwhile, the Colorado businesses will not be able to ship their goods efficiently because they will face a shortage of trains, and they will lose money as well. Meanwhile, Rearden cannot possibly meet the demands of the new laws. One requires him to limit his output of Rearden Metal, while another requires him to sell a "fair share" of Rearden Metal to everyone who requests it, regardless of output. Rand demonstrates how a society that controls its economy through harsh regulations eventually creates new criminals by creating new crimes. Rearden is made a criminal under one set of laws to meet the requirements of another. To the rational mind, these outcomes are obvious, but since the looters have rejected reason and rationality, they cannot see the long-term issues.

The story of Lee Hunsacker, Midas Mulligan, and Judge Narragansett further illustrates the irrational nature of socialist laws and offers some clues about the motives of the men who have disappeared. Although he had believed he was following noble socialist ideals, the judge who overturned Narragansett's ruling created an impossibly absurd situation. By ordering Mulligan to issue a loan to Hunsacker precisely because of Hunsacker's need and, more importantly, his inability to repay it, the judge had allowed the doctrine of need to triumph over reason. In response to this, Mulligan and Narragansett have retired and disappeared, just like the industrialists. Dagny gets more clues to the motives behind the disappearances when she finds Hugh Akston. He retired because he could no longer practice as a philosopher. Since his philosophy is the philosophy of reason, only reason could have pulled him away from the world. To live in the world as Dagny and Rearden live—under the yoke of weak, malicious men—presented to Akston and the others some fundamental logical contradiction. Though its full nature has not yet been revealed, the force at work among the nation's vanishing industrialists may simply be the force of reason.

Part Two, Chapters I–II

Summary — Chapter I: The Man Who Belonged on Earth

Dagny must cut trains from her schedules as Colorado's economy collapses. No one is able to draw oil from Wyatt's fields, and companies that depended on his oil go out of business. With severe oil shortages and government rationing, much of the country turns to coal. But Andrew Stockton, a maker of coal furnaces who stands to make a fortune, has mysteriously vanished. Lawrence Hammond is gone as well. He had been the last car manufacturer. Ken Dannager, of Dannager Coal, is one of the few industrialists left. The only Taggart train running on oil is the Taggart Comet, its transcontinental flagship, but all others are running on coal. Taggart is pulling less and less every day, but Jim has acquired a stream of subsidies from Washington that keep Taggart profits at an all-time high.

Dagny has intensified her quest to rebuild the motor. She calls Robert Stadler, hoping he can help her find an engineer. When she shows him what she has, he is amazed at the mind that created it. He wonders why such a pure mind would be concerned with such mundane things as motors. He recommends a physicist named Quentin Daniels, a brilliant man who had refused to work at the State Science Institute.

The Fair Share Law dictates that Rearden must supply metal to all who ask, but there is no way to meet all the orders. Men with influence manage to acquire much more than their "fair share," while legitimate orders go unfilled. The government sends a young man to the mills to work as Deputy Director of Distribution and determine the amounts of orders. The steelworkers call him "the Wet Nurse." Rearden chooses to ignore an order from the State Science Institute for something called Project X. A week later, a man from the Institute comes to see Rearden. He tries to convince Rearden to acquiesce, but Rearden refuses. Rearden tells the representative to bring in trucks and steal as much metal as the Institute needs, but he will not help Washington pretend that he is a willing seller. The man seems frightened. He issues some vague threats and leaves. Afterwards, Rearden begins to realize the looters need his sanction, which he must never give.

SUMMARY — CHAPTER II: THE ARISTOCRACY OF PULL

Dagny begins to believe that a destroyer is at work, removing the smartest and most talented industrialists. Nearly every business-man in Colorado is gone. Dagny feels that she must fight this force, whatever it is. She hires Quentin Daniels, the man Stadler recommended, to work at reconstructing the motor. In a furtive meeting, Rearden arranges to sell Ken Dannager a larger order of Rearden Metal than the law allows.

Jim marries Cherryl Brooks at a gala wedding party. Although he does not want to go, Rearden agrees to accompany his wife. Lillian tells Jim her gift is bringing Rearden, because now others will think Rearden is scared of Jim, which will help Jim's reputation. At the wedding, Lillian notices Dagny wearing the Rearden Metal bracelet and asks for it back, but Dagny refuses. Lillian vaguely suggests that Dagny may be inviting conjecture by wearing it. When Dagny asks her directly if she means to imply that she and Rearden are having an affair, Lillian denies it. Rearden, standing nearby, demands that she apologize to Dagny. Both women are shocked. After some hesitation, Lillian offers an apology. Rearden once stood by his wife, but now he stands by Dagny.

Francisco d'Anconia is also at the party. Upon hearing a remark that money is the root of all evil, and d'Anconia is its typical product, Francisco replies with an astounding dissertation on the true role of money. Money, he says, is the antithesis of evil and in fact represents the greatest good. Francisco tells Rearden that there is no evil except the refusal to think and that this is precisely the mistake Rearden is making by living as he does. He wants to show Rearden the alternative. Tomorrow morning, he says, the holders of d'Anconia stock will discover that nearly every mine has been destroyed as a result of poor management. D'Anconia stock will collapse. Francisco's comments create a panic in the room, as many guests, especially Jim, will lose huge investments.

ANALYSIS: PART TWO, CHAPTERS I–II

Dr. Stadler sees science as the abstract realm of pure thought, but for Dagny, science serves the practical needs of life. Humans are fundamentally irrational in Stadler's thinking, so any application of science to human life is equally irrational. In response to the motor, he wonders why any mind so purely brilliant could be interested in the mundane, practical application of his discoveries. Dagny, on the other hand, assumes that the inventor created a practical tool because he liked life and "belonged on Earth." The inventor, like Dagny, understood the role of thought in man's happiness on Earth. He did not believe in the separation of thought and action or mind and body, but believed in their integration. This integration is a critical feature of Rand's philosophy, which holds that rational thought cannot be separated from the things it creates or the world it powers.

The Wet Nurse embodies the collectivist world in which he was trained. Although he has a degree in metallurgy, he has no practical skills. He merely repeats things he has been told and uses words cleverly so as not to say anything clearly. He is taken aback by

Rearden's insistence on calling things exactly what they are. His job is to determine Rearden's output so that it is in compliance with the laws. But without the laws, there would be no need for his job in the first place. Rand, a strong proponent of unfettered capitalism, uses him to demonstrate the absurd ways in which bureaucracy fuels its own growth and the waste and foolishness required to keep an artificial system running. In a capitalist system, Rearden would be free to produce as much steel as his customers require, and they would be free to buy it or to go elsewhere if he could not give them what they wanted. For Rand, the simplicity of free markets stands in obvious contrast to the complex bureaucratic structures seen here.

Jim's wedding offers more insight into the back-door intrigue that runs the looters' world. Everyone at the party falls into one of two categories: those who have come as a favor to Jim and those who have come in fear of his hostility. The first group consists mostly of Washington men, the second mostly of businessmen. The sum of the two groups is an estimation of Jim's power. Their complicated web of influence is based solely on each man's connection to the ultimate power in the decaying nation: physical force. Though everyone knows this, no one is willing to admit it. The bare, ugly truth of their power hides behind a mask of words and euphemisms. Francisco reveals the fragility of this illusion when he asks if any of them realize that to destroy their entire complex structure, it would only take someone naming the exact nature of what they are doing. This line offers a useful piece of foreshadowing.

Francisco's "money speech" lays out some critical elements of Rand's philosophy. In it, he puts forth the idea that rather than being the root of evil, money is the manifestation of creativity and good. Money is exchanged for and represents the products and services created by man. Creative production makes survival and prosperity possible and is therefore the highest good. If a man's ability to be productive is represented by his ability to make money, then money is a moral tool and an indicator of the value of man. Another key element of Rand's philosophy demonstrated here is the necessity of accepting and stating what is real. For Rand, as for Francisco, the only evil is the refusal to think. The looters' success depends on their victims refusing to see or confront what is happening. But the heroes—Dagny, Rearden, and Francisco—will not go along. They insist on clarity and straight speaking, which rattles the looters, who are themselves in denial.

Finally, the altercation between Dagny and Lillian marks a growing change in Rearden. He has already begun to understand that he cannot be victimized without giving his sanction to his victimizers. When he tells the representative from the State Science Institute that he will not pretend to be a willing seller but will force them act as the thieves they really are, he understands his own power in his business affairs. When Dagny refuses to go along with Lillian's vague accusations but forces her to be specific, Rearden sees that Lillian also requires the sanction of her victim. He stands by Dagny now, just as he stood by Lillian previously. He has begun, slowly, to integrate his public and private selves and understand his power. Meanwhile, Francisco continues to counsel him and arm him with moral clarity.

PART TWO, CHAPTERS III–IV

SUMMARY — CHAPTER III: WHITE BLACKMAIL
After the party, Rearden goes to see Dagny and asks her to forgive him for coming with Lillian. He tells her that what he said at Wyatt's house was wrong. Dagny has always known this, and she tells him there is nothing to forgive. Meanwhile, Lillian discovers that Rearden has a mistress, but she does not know who it is.

Dr. Floyd Ferris of the State Science Institute comes to see Rearden and tells him that if he will not fill the order for Project X, he will be arrested for his illegal deal with Ken Dannager. Rearden refuses, and both Rearden and Dannager are indicted.

Eddie Willers eats lunch with his worker friend. He worries about Dagny. She knows that Rearden is strong enough to stand trial, but she is afraid for Dannager. She thinks he is ready to break and will be taken by the destroyer. He tells the worker Dagny is going to see Dannager tomorrow afternoon. When Dagny reaches Dannager's office, she is too late. He is with a visitor, and when he finally meets with her, he has already decided to retire. He assures her that even if she had reached him before his last visitor, she would not have been able to prevent his retirement. His only real regret is that he is leaving Rearden behind at such a dangerous time.

Francisco comes to see Rearden at his mill. He asks Rearden why he is willing to accept condemnation for his virtues and sanction the actions of his enemies. Francisco tells Rearden his only sin is to agree that his self-interest is wrong. Rearden should have reaped incredible benefits from his invention, but instead he is punished for it. His hard work has only empowered the looters. Francisco asks Rearden what would he say if he saw Atlas holding the weight of the world but losing strength. Rearden asks what Francisco would tell him to do. "To shrug," Francisco answers. Rearden begins to think he understands Francisco. Francisco is about to ask Rearden what makes him continue his work, when suddenly an alarm rings and they must rush to fix a broken furnace. They work with skill and speed, each knowing exactly what to do. Afterwards, Rearden asks if Francisco wishes to continue his question. Francisco tells him that he knows now exactly why Rearden remains with his mills.

SUMMARY—CHAPTER IV: THE SANCTION OF THE VICTIM
At Thanksgiving dinner with his family, Rearden begins to see them in a new light. He finally confronts his brother Philip, who has sponged off of him for years without respecting him, and tells him he no longer cares what happens to him. He realizes that he has allowed his family to inflict suffering on him by accepting their condemnation. He will no longer offer them his sanction by accepting their moral code over his own.

At his trial, Rearden refuses to participate. He offers no defense because he refuses to honor the proceedings or pretend the trial has merit. He declares that he does not recognize the court's right to control the sale of his metal. He explains that he lives for the sake of creation and profit and that he refuses to apologize for his success. The crowd bursts into applause behind him. The judges are frightened and apologetic. They impose a $5,000 fine on him but suspend the sentence.

Rearden goes to see d'Anconia at his hotel in New York. When he asks how a man as intelligent as Francisco could waste time in promiscuity, Francisco begins a discussion of sex, saying that a man's lover is the embodiment of his moral code. If he despises himself, he will pursue immoral women. If he truly knows his own worth, he will seek a goddess. Though he has purposely fueled the scandals surrounding his own love life, Francisco has loved only one woman in his life.

Rearden tells him that he has decided to sell his metal to whomever he wants and has ordered copper directly from d'Anconia. Francisco shouts he had warned Rearden not to deal with d'Anconia copper and runs to the phone, but stops himself. He turns to Rearden and swears by the woman he loves that he is his friend, though Rearden will soon damn him. Days later, Rearden learns

that the ships bearing his copper were seized and sunk by the pirate
Ragnar Danneskjold.

ANALYSIS: PART TWO, CHAPTERS III–IV

Rearden represents the mythical Atlas of whom Francisco speaks.
He has been carrying the world and is now being punished for it. But
he is no longer a willing participant in his own victimization. He has
rejected the division of mind and body, and admitted to Dagny that
his attitude toward sex has been misguided. He has confronted his
family and put them on notice that they can no longer use his own
sense of honor as a weapon against him. Most important, he has
confronted the politicians who accuse him of breaking an irrational
and unjust law. He triumphs at his trial because he withdraws his
sanction. He refuses to help the politicians hide the brute force that
is the true nature of their power. He tells the politicians, "If you
believe that you have the right to force me—use your guns openly. I
will not help you to disguise the nature of your action." By exposing
them for what they are, Rearden has upset the system in which the
looters exploit their victims' refusal to see reality. The looters need
Rearden to work so they can feed off his productivity, so they are
forced to set him free. In this, the essential paradox of collectivism is
revealed. The strong are tyrannized by the weak and made to feel
obligated to support them, but only their belief that they must allow
it keeps them shackled. If they refuse to participate, if "Atlas
shrugs," the weak will have no recourse beyond brute strength.
While people can use physical violence to coerce action, they cannot
force others to think or create for them.

Rearden's transformation continues to be fueled by Francisco's
wise counseling. In their conversation at the mills, Rearden is closer
than ever to understanding the message Francisco offers him. Francisco is on the verge of revealing more to Rearden and finally
explaining why he must destroy his own fortune, when the fire inter-
rupts them. Afterward, Francisco cannot continue. He knows that
Rearden's love for his work will continue to hold him. When
Rearden's copper supply is hijacked by Ragnar Danneskjold, he
knows Francisco is behind the attack. The betrayal means the loss of
Francisco's friendship as well.

After Dannager retires, Dagny knows that the disappearance of
the industrialists is not a random coincidence. The timing of the disappearances is deliberate as well. Stockton disappeared just as the
need for his furnaces intensified. Now Dannager is gone at the very

moment his coal becomes essential. She is convinced a destroyer is loose on the world, deliberately snatching great men just as they are needed most. But many questions remain. Dagny must find out who the destroyer is and how he knows which men to take. Furthermore, if the vanished men are alive, where have they gone?

PART TWO, CHAPTERS V–VI

SUMMARY — CHAPTER V: ACCOUNT OVERDRAWN

John Galt is Prometheus who changed his mind.
(*See* QUOTATIONS, *p. 68*)

The order for Taggart rail is the first failure in the history of Rearden Steel. Without the copper, there is nothing Rearden can do, and without the metal, Taggart cannot fix its crumbling mainline track. There are more accidents, and shippers who cannot get goods through go out of business. The economy spirals quickly downward.

Colorado has become destitute, and virtually no businesses remain on the Rio Norte Line. At a board meeting, Dagny is forced to close the line and use the Rearden Metal to repair the worst problems on the main line. A representative from Washington tells Jim that in order to get the permits he needs, he will have to offer Wesley Mouch something. As she leaves the meeting, Dagny finds Francisco D'Anconia waiting for her. He asks her how long she is willing to continue working for people who do not deserve her. She tells him that whatever the cost, she cannot abandon the railroad.

Jim Taggart finds himself pulled in different directions by the politicians and looters, and must find something valuable to use to curry favor. The government wants no trouble from Rearden when they announce another new law, so Jim seeks information about Rearden that might help. He asks Lillian Rearden to dinner. She agrees to help. After some investigation, Lillian discovers that Dagny is Rearden's mistress. When she confronts him, Rearden refuses to end the affair, saying he would sooner see Lillian dead.

SUMMARY — CHAPTER VI: MIRACLE METAL

Wesley Mouch, Jim Taggart, Orren Boyle, Dr. Floyd Ferris, Mr. Weatherby, Fred Kinnan (head of the Amalgamated Labor of America), and Mr. Thompson (the Head of State) meet to discuss Directive 10-289. This set of laws is designed to freeze the economy in its present state and prevent further decline. Although they fear the public's response, they vote to enact the laws.

According to the directive, workers must remain in their present jobs or face prison, and all businesses must remain in operation. All patents and copyrights must be turned over to the government by means of voluntary Gift Certificates. No new devices, inventions, or products can be produced. Every company is required to produce the same amount of goods as the previous year, no more and no less. Wages and prices are to be frozen, and every citizen is required to spend the same amount of money as in the previous year. All research departments must close except for the State Science Institute. To oversee the law, the Bureau of Economic Planning appoints a Unification Board, whose rulings are final.

Dr. Ferris notes that Hank Rearden will fight them for his patent, but Jim assures Mouch that he can control Rearden in exchange for Mouch's raising his freight rates before the directive freezes all prices.

Along with many other people around the country, Dagny immediately resigns when she learns of the directive. She goes away to a lodge she owns in the country. Dozens of industrialists disappear. Even the Wet Nurse is outraged at what the government has done. He has not been reporting Rearden's illegal activities. His work at the mills has made him begin to reject the ideologies he has been taught. Dr. Floyd Ferris comes to see Rearden to demand he sign over the patent for Rearden Metal, now to be called "Miracle Metal." When Rearden refuses, Ferris shows him evidence of his affair with Dagny and threatens to ruin Dagny's reputation by making it public. He tells Rearden it was Lillian who sold him out. Rearden blames himself for not divorcing Lillian and making his relationship with Dagny legitimate. But he cannot see her destroyed, so he signs.

ANALYSIS: PART TWO, CHAPTERS V–VI

The country's economic decline is the logical result of recent events. In a vast ripple effect, the problems are compounded. A lack of copper means Rearden cannot make his metal. As a result, Taggart cannot fix broken track and must run limited service. This leads to shippers losing customers, causing them to go bankrupt, leaving Taggart with fewer customers, forcing them to make further cuts in service, and so on. Everything in an economic system is connected. By outlining these related failures, Rand demonstrates how interference in any part of an economy has consequences on every other part of it. To Rand, the only legitimate role for government in an economic system is noninterference.

The politicians seem surprised at the spiraling economy and never entertain the idea that their policies may be to blame. As consummate bureaucrats, their only response is to enact even more policies, culminating in the overreaching Directive 10-289. The absurd act is riddled with contradictions and double-speak, such as the order that inventors be compelled to "voluntarily" give up their patents. In blindly piling irrational law upon irrational law, the politicians reveal their unwillingness to see the reality before them. They have become so used to feeding off the productive elements in society that they have not noticed that these elements are no longer there. Among the looters, only the Wet Nurse can see how insane the directive really is. He has begun to see that the ideas he believed in were absurd. For some time, he has been keeping Rearden's illegal activities to himself, partly out of personal admiration for Rearden. Now he can no longer support the system he has been part of. The Wet Nurse is a notable character in that he is the only one of the looters to have such a realization and to accept the reality of what is happening.

Rearden's transformation is nearly complete. He now understands that he follows the code of life and creative production while the looters, by seeking to destroy his ability to produce, follow a code of death. By allowing them to ensnare him in their false, self-sacrificing morality, he has unwittingly helped them. This knowledge is liberating for him, but there is one more price he must pay. He knows now that his affair with Dagny is a noble and good thing, and he wishes he had been free enough to see it sooner. He does not care how the public views him, but he will not allow Dagny to pay the price for his mistake. He signs the Gift Certificate to protect her, but it is the last time he will do anything to help the looters.

PART TWO, CHAPTERS VII–VIII

SUMMARY—CHAPTER VII: THE MORATORIUM ON BRAINS

Eddie Willers meets his worker friend at the Taggart cafeteria. He complains about the terrible effect of the directive on the railroad. Competent men are abandoning their posts, and only shiftless vagrants are taking jobs. A friend of Jim's, Clifton Locey, has been hired to replace Dagny. His sole purpose each day is to avoid making decisions. The worker tells Eddie that he will not be coming back the next week because he is going away for a month's vacation.

Rearden has moved out of his house and asked his lawyers to pull whatever strings are necessary to obtain a divorce from Lillian with no financial settlement for her. Walking to his apartment one night, he meets a man dressed in dark clothes who calls himself the friend of the friendless and hands Rearden a bar of solid gold. He tells Rearden that the gold is partial repayment for the income taxes he has been paying to a corrupt government, and it represents justice. He has been collecting the taxes of many industrialists for years in order to help them rebuild the world after the looters force it to collapse. When Rearden learns that the man is Ragnar Danneskjold, he is appalled, but moments later lies to police to protect him.

Taggart's cross-country Comet is stranded in Colorado. Kip Chalmers, an important politician, is on board and demands that the train move ahead. The diesel engine is beyond repair, and the only available replacement is coal-burning and cannot enter the long, airless Taggart Tunnel. After a series of communications in which everyone from Jim Taggart to the train's engineer refuses to take responsibility by sending vague directives, Chalmers is finally able to bully the employees into using the coal engine. A drunken engineer agrees to take the Comet through the tunnel after the assigned engineer resigns in protest. Everyone on board is killed from the toxic fumes. The last thing they see is the still-burning flame of Wyatt's oil fields ("Wyatt's Torch"). Later, an army munitions train slams into the stalled Comet and explodes, destroying the tunnel.

SUMMARY — CHAPTER VIII: BY OUR LOVE

Francisco visits Dagny at her country lodge. He has come to confess his love and tell her everything. Now that she has quit, he thinks she is ready to join him. He tells her that he is one of the industrialists who have withdrawn from the world. But instead of disappearing like the others, he has stayed and systematically ruined d'Anconia Copper to keep the looters from taking it. She is furious that he could do such dishonor to something he loved so much, but he tells her that it was for the sake of his love that he did what he did. Losing her respect was the hardest part.

Dagny begins to see the logic of Francisco's withdrawal and is ready to follow him when the radio broadcasts the news of the tunnel disaster. Instinctively, she rushes back to her job. She restores train service by rerouting onto other railroads' tracks. Her actions are illegal under the Directive, but she knows the Unification Board will not stop her, as they now depend on her to fix the problem. She calls Rearden and admits she knows the looters are using her love for her railroad to hold her captive, just as they hold Rearden for his love of his work.

ANALYSIS: PART TWO, CHAPTERS VII–VIII

By now we know that the worker Eddie dines with in the Taggart cafeteria is a key figure in the story, but still we know nothing about him. In a novel filled with dialogue, he himself has no lines. Everything he says is inferred from Eddie's responses. This curious fact highlights the mystery of who he is and why he is so interested in Eddie's stories. Whoever he is, he knows a great deal about Dagny from his conversations with Eddie.

The mysterious Ragnar Danneskjold is finally revealed, and Francisco's mysteries also become clear. On meeting Danneskjold, Rearden finds him to be a thoughtful and articulate man with a rational approach to his activities, far from the criminal thug Rearden imagined. Danneskjold represents justice in the story as he seeks to right the wrongs committed by the looters. In order to fight for justice, he must become a criminal, which is ironic, but when robbery is sanctioned by law, restitution becomes a crime. Although Rearden has always despised Danneskjold, after learning Danneskjold's true story, Rearden is compelled to protect him from the police. The gold Danneskjold gives Rearden becomes a source of strength for him as the chaos intensifies.

As for Francisco, we learn he is one of the vanished businessmen, but he has chosen to stay in the looters' world to further its collapse and urge others to withdraw. His conversations with Rearden and Dagny have been part of his recruiting effort. When he tells everything to Dagny, he nearly succeeds in getting her to leave, to withdraw her mind and ability in order to speed up the inevitable collapse of society. But in the same way that the furnace fire pulled Rearden back to his mills, the tunnel disaster pulls Dagny back to her railroad, just when she was ready to leave it. Dagny and Rearden both know they are held to the corrupt system by their love for their work. They know they are helping to feed the parasites, but their love is still too compelling.

With no one of substance or intelligence left in leadership roles, the Taggart Tunnel disaster is inevitable. Dagny would have let rational facts rule her decision and would never have allowed the train to enter the tunnel, regardless of the consequences for her. But Clifton Locey's only concern is his own place in the hierarchy of influence and favor. He refuses to upset a powerful Washington man, even if his refusal ultimately kills the man. Although he will not say no to running the coal train, he is also very careful not to say yes either. The fear of taking responsibility is a characteristic shared by all of the looters. The issue of personal responsibility is critical to Rand's philosophy. Her heroes are always decisive and responsible regardless of the situations they face.

Part Two, Chapters IX–X

Summary — Chapter IX: The Face Without Pain or Fear or Guilt

Francisco comes to Dagny's apartment to try again to convince her to quit, but she cannot give up the railroad. Suddenly, Rearden enters the apartment. He sees Francisco and is furious. Francisco is stunned to see that Dagny is sleeping with Rearden. Rearden remembers Francisco's oath of love to one woman and asks if Dagny is the one. When Francisco says yes, Rearden slaps him. It takes all the self-restraint Francisco can manage not to retaliate, and Rearden realizes how much this man loves him. Francisco concedes that based on what he knows, Rearden is still correct in denouncing him. He leaves the apartment.

Dagny receives a letter from Quentin Daniels, who is resigning. Although he will still work on the motor, he will not accept her money, since he does not want the motor to be used by the looters. Dagny calls him and makes him promise to wait for her to come and see him. She calls Eddie and tells him to hold the Comet for her. She will go west to look into the tunnel accident and to find Daniels.

Eddie comes to Dagny's apartment to get instructions while she packs. When he sees Rearden's dressing gown in her closet, he is stunned to realize they are lovers and that he has also been in love with Dagny for years. Later, he goes to eat dinner at the Taggart Cafeteria with the worker. He tells him that he has always liked his face because it looks like the face of a man who has never known pain or fear or guilt. He tells him Dagny is going to find Quentin Daniels and also tells him about the motor. When he mentions his love for Dagny and his shock at learning about her and Rearden, the worker hurries away.

SUMMARY: CHAPTER X: THE SIGN OF THE DOLLAR

Dagny is shaken by the desolation she passes as she rides west on the Comet. As she steps out of her private car, she sees a conductor removing a hobo from the vestibule. Something in his dignity strikes her, and she invites him in. His name is Jeff Allen, and he used to work for the Twentieth Century Motor Company. He tells her the story of what happened at the plant when Starnes's heirs began their disastrous policies. Every six months, the workers would come together to vote on each person's needs. If it was decided that anyone was not producing enough, that man was made to work extra unpaid hours. Eventually, all the workers lost their dignity. The honest men were punished, and the rest learned to manipulate the system and hide their abilities. The first man to quit was named John Galt. He swore he would end the absurdity and stop the motor of the world. After the factory closings and failures that followed, Allen and his coworkers began to think he had succeeded, and they coined the phrase *Who is John Galt?*

The train stops suddenly. Like many trains lately, it has been deserted by its crew, who simply disappear. Dagny is relieved to find Owen Kellogg on the train, but he is on his way to a month's vacation and will not help, though he does accompany her to a track phone to call for help. On the way, he asks her why she continues to work for the looters even now. He also smokes the mysterious cigarettes stamped with the dollar sign. Dagny continues on to a nearby airstrip, where she rents a plane. When she lands, she learns that Quentin Daniels has just taken off in another plane. Fearing the destroyer has taken him, she takes off and follows them. She crashes in the remote Colorado mountains.

ANALYSIS: PART TWO, CHAPTERS IX–X

The scene in Dagny's apartment illustrates how much Francisco has had to give up to follow his mission and how important it is to him. Not only has he given up on d'Anconia Copper and allowed his personal reputation to be destroyed, he has given up the only woman he ever loved and betrayed Rearden, a man he loves and respects. The strength required to stay on his course in the face of all he has lost is illustrated in the moment after Rearden slaps him and he does not retaliate, instead acknowledging that Rearden is right to denounce him. Whatever he is accomplishing by withdrawing from the looters' world must be very important indeed.

We can now be certain that the track worker with whom Eddie dines must be connected to the destroyer in some way. It is no coincidence that Daniels (and earlier, Dannager) disappeared immediately after Eddie happened to mention to the track worker Dagny's plans to try to stop them. Furthermore, the worker's interest in Dagny seems personal, given his abrupt reaction to learning she and Rearden are lovers.

Rand uses Jeff Allen's detailed account of the chaos at the Twentieth Century Motor Company to illustrate the devastating effects of collectivism. For Rand, the ideas behind the plant's radical management are not just bad ideas, they are pure evil. She intends the plant's story to be an object lesson in the perils of Communism. Under the system at the plant, income was based on need, not performance. Using need as a basis for policy is the system's fundamental flaw, for a number of reasons. First, need has no absolute definitions; what is a need to one person may be a luxury to another. Second, rewarding income based on need removes incentive. If production is separated from income, there is no reason to produce, since a worker will receive income anyway. Finally, ability becomes a liability when those determined to be ablest are given more work but not more income. The biggest winner under such a system is the person with the most need and the least ability. This fact makes it inevitable that a community should dissolve into chaos and mistrust, and that production should cease. From Jeff Allen, Dagny also learns the true story of John Galt. She now knows that he is a real person and that he was the first to resign from the plant. His vow to "stop the motor of the world" indicates that he may be the destroyer she seeks. He may also be the inventor of the motor. She is more determined than ever to find him.

PART THREE, CHAPTERS I–II

SUMMARY—CHAPTER I: ATLANTIS

> *I swear by my life and my love of it that I will never live for the sake of another man, nor ask another man to live for mine.*
>
> (*See* QUOTATIONS, *p. 69*)

Dagny opens her eyes and looks into the face of a man—a face that bears no mark of pain or fear or guilt. His name is John Galt, and he had been the pilot of the plane she followed. He is the man Jeff Allen described. He is also the inventor of the motor and the destroyer Dagny has feared. She has injured her ankle. He carries her away from the wreckage. On the way to his house, Dagny discovers that this remote mountain valley is the home of all the vanished industrialists. The banker Midas Mulligan owns the valley. Hugh Akston, the composer Richard Halley, Judge Narragansett, and many others who have disappeared are all living here. Francisco is also, not surprisingly, a member of the community.

The industrialists have all built businesses, and the valley is self-sufficient. Galt's motor powers the electricity as well as a special ray screen that hides the valley from the rest of the world. When Galt takes Dagny to see the building where the motor is kept, she reads an inscription above the door: "I swear by my life and my love of it that I will never live for the sake of another man, nor ask another man to live for mine." This is the oath of the valley, and until a person will say it and mean it, he or she cannot live there.

At a dinner at Mulligan's home, Galt explains to Dagny that they are all on strike. The only men who have never gone on strike in human history, he tells her, are the men who bear the world on their shoulders. All other laborers have at one point or another presented demands to the world. This, he tells her, is the mind on strike.

SUMMARY — CHAPTER II: THE UTOPIA OF GREED

The next morning, Dagny meets the pirate Ragnar Danneskjold, who lives in the valley. He has come for breakfast with Galt and Francisco, who has not arrived yet. Although many of the strikers live in the valley, others, like Francisco, go back and forth to the looters' world. But every June, all the members of the community spend the month in the valley together. Dagny agrees to stay the month and then decide if she will remain. Although Danneskjold has created an account for her at Mulligan's bank, she refuses to use the money and instead agrees to work as Galt's maid to earn her keep.

Owen Kellogg arrives on Dagny's third day in the valley. He tells her that everyone in the outside world thinks she is dead, including Rearden. The next day Francisco d'Anconia arrives at Galt's home. He has been searching for Dagny's plane for days and is shocked and overjoyed when he sees her. He tells her he loves her and knows she will always love him, even if she belongs to another man. Galt forbids any outside communication, so Dagny cannot get word to Rearden that she is safe.

Dagny comes to realize that she is in love with Galt and that he loves her too. He is the man she has always imagined finding. He admits he has watched her from afar for years. Since they are still on opposite sides of the strike, she fears they cannot be together. She also fears Galt will hide his feelings out of concern for Francisco, who still loves her. When Francisco invites her to his home, she turns the question over to Galt, who tells her he wants her to stay with him instead. Galt knows this was a test and that by not descending to self-sacrifice, he has passed. He reminds Dagny that no one stays in the valley under any pretense or emotional shield.

Despite her great happiness in the valley, Dagny decides she must return to fight for her railroad. Against the warnings of his friends, Galt decides to return as well, to watch her and wait for her to be ready to return. She promises to keep the secret of the valley and is escorted out blindfolded and flown to the outside world.

ANALYSIS: PART THREE, CHAPTERS I–II

In her description of the valley, Rand presents her ideal world. In it, men and women with creative, productive minds live in a self-sufficient community where innovation is encouraged and property and money are respected. All the members of the community are egoists, meaning they are focused on themselves and on seeking their own happiness through the exercise of their unique talents. Men have no moral obligations to each other except to respect the individual rights of others. Everyone takes responsibility for themselves, their actions, and their decisions, and there are no pretenses or false realities—everything is as it seems. The oath the strikers live by is Rand's own oath and a cornerstone of her philosophy, the philosophy of the ego.

The mysteries that have driven the novel so far are finally solved. Dagny has found everything she was looking for in John Galt: the destroyer, the inventor of the motor, and her life's love. We now understand what Francisco was trying to explain all along and why the great thinkers have all come here. Even the identity of Eddie's mysterious friend is now clear. We know from the description of Galt as having "a face without pain or fear or guilt" that he must be the track worker, since this is the exact description Eddie had used. Furthermore, Galt claims he has watched Dagny every day for years, which would only be possible if he worked nearby. But since Dagny doesn't know about Eddie's friend, she is still unaware that Galt is her employee.

The mind on strike is a central theme of *Atlas Shrugged*. To Rand, the mind provides the motive power of the world. The ability to think rationally and to apply rational thought in creative production makes man's happiness and success possible. The rational mind is behind every idea and invention that has moved civilization forward. Without the mind, men are plunged into chaos and cease to produce. The strike of the mind is no mere concept, but a real action that has had serious consequences. The withdrawal of the strikers' minds hastened the destruction of civil society and brought the looters closer to their eventual oblivion. This strike is very different from most and throws the logic of labor strikes on its head. As Galt points out, strikes throughout history have been of laborers, and the argument has been that manual labor is the true source of wealth, exploited by industrialists. But Galt's strike proves that the thinkers are the ones responsible for prosperity. Manual laborers still remain in the looters' world, but since the guidance of the thinkers has been withdrawn, they don't know what to do and cannot make progress.

The strikers are sure that the looters cannot change and must be allowed to destroy themselves, but Dagny still believes there is a chance. She thinks the looters are capable of rational thought and will ultimately recognize their errors and step aside for people like her and Rearden to fix the problems they have created. While there is still a chance, she must return to the world. Galt is sure the looters will never be able to look directly at the reality they inhabit and will evade the truth until the end. He is sure that end is coming soon and wants to be near Dagny when she sees it too.

PART THREE, CHAPTERS III–IV

SUMMARY — CHAPTER III: ANTI-GREED

In rural Iowa, the government unveils the Thompson Harmonizer, a new super-weapon, the result of the mysterious Project X. Although he has known nothing of it, Dr. Robert Stadler finds himself being credited with its creation and coerced to speak at the unveiling event. The weapon uses sound waves to destroy all living things within its radius. Dr. Floyd Ferris convinces him it is necessary to control an increasingly hysterical population. The stunned and horrified audience watches as a farmhouse and some goats are torn to shreds by the machine, but no one comments. Wesley Mouch declares it to be a wonderful instrument of peace.

Dagny calls Rearden to tell him she is alive. When she returns to the office, she learns that the government has passed the Railroad Unification Plan. Under it, all the railroads will pool profits and distribute them according to the mileage of track each railroad maintains. Taggart stands to make a huge profit because it owns the most track. Eddie is meeting with Cuffy Meigs, the head of the Unification Board, who is in charge of the new plan. Under his orders, trains are being rerouted and used as favors for influential friends.

Jim insists that Dagny appear on a radio show that night to reassure the public that she has not deserted and that the railroads are safe. She refuses. Later, Lillian visits her and tells her that her affair with Rearden will be exposed if she does no go on the air. She agrees to appear. When she speaks on the air, she proudly tells the public about her affair with Rearden and about the blackmail used to force him to sign over the rights to Rearden Metal. When she sees Rearden later that night, he finally confesses his love for her, although he already knows he has lost her to the man she truly loves. Her speech on the radio had been delivered in the past tense. When she tells him that her love's name is John Galt, he is astonished. He suspects where she has been.

SUMMARY — CHAPTER IV: ANTI-LIFE

Jim Taggart is pleased with a deal he has just arranged. Argentina has been declared a People's State, and d'Anconia Copper will be nationalized in less than a month. Knowing this in advance, Taggart transfers his investments from d'Anconia Copper to a new company, which will control its assets after the nationalization. Aware that he will make a fortune he feels a vague desire to celebrate. He hopes that his wife, Cherryl, will give him the admiration he seeks, but she is no longer in awe of him, having realized his true nature in the year since their wedding. She has learned the true story of the John Galt Line, and suspects some terrible evil in Jim. When he drinks a toast to destroying Francisco, she leaves in disgust.

Cherryl goes to see Dagny. She offers an apology for accusing Dagny of being the weak and evil one at Taggart. She knows now it was Dagny who created all the success and Jim who was wrong. Dagny accepts her apology and offers to help Cherryl. She talks about the evil of giving to the undeserving and about the importance of justice, and Cherryl finally feels she is understood.

Back at Jim's apartment, Lillian Rearden appears. She has come to ask Jim to use his influence to prevent Rearden from divorcing her, but he cannot help her. In a final attempt to hurt Rearden, she has emotionless sex with Jim.

When Cherryl returns, it is clear Jim has been unfaithful. He admits it and says he will never give her a divorce, and she is stuck with him. She asks why he married her. He tells her viciously that he married her because she was worthless, because he wanted her to accept his love as alms. She realizes that he really married her because she was struggling to rise above the gutter, and it was this struggle he wanted to destroy. She tells him he is a killer for the sake of killing, and he slaps her. She runs out into the street, where a social worker sees her and tells her that her despair is a result of her selfishness. This is too much to take, and she jumps off a bridge and drowns.

ANALYSIS: PART THREE, CHAPTERS III–IV

Project X reveals the extent to which the looters' regime depends on sheer brute force. The monstrous machine, built using scientific principles discovered by Dr. Stadler, demonstrates what is created when the mind is used by the state for its own ends. With the machine at its disposal, the government has become a true dictatorship, able to dominate its people through threats and violence. Stadler's willingness to participate in the unveiling marks the final collapse of his integrity. He has known nothing of the project and realizes that his name is being associated with it to make the public more accepting. At first, he is outraged at being used and horrified by the machine itself, but he does as he is told, even agreeing to read the speech prepared for him by the government. He now stands fully with the looters.

The Railroad Unification plan is another example of the absurd efforts of the government. But this time there is no effort to even hide the absurdity or pretend that the good of the nation will be served. The plan benefits only Taggart Transcontinental and the well-connected Jim Taggart, who is credited with delivering Rearden to the looters. Taggart has been using the tracks of other railroads to get around the destroyed tunnel but is not responsible for maintaining them. Meanwhile, Taggart owns more track than anyone, but most of it is unused. By crafting the plan to reward income based on amount of track owned instead of service provided, Taggart will reap huge profits. Smaller railroads will maintain the lines it is using, and its own lines will carry almost no traffic. The most successful railroad under the plan would be one that owns the most track but runs no trains at all.

Dagny's radio address is a triumph of reason and honesty over deceit and denial. At first, she refuses to appear because to do so would imply her endorsement of the Railroad Unification Plan and would suggest the industry is not in shambles. Both would be lies. But when she learns of the blackmail used on Rearden, she welcomes the opportunity to avenge him. She is not bothered by publicly revealing her affair with Rearden. As she has said before, she is proud of it, and her own opinion is the only one that matters to her. Dagny does not believe in the separation of the mind and body that would make her physical desires base and shameful. For her, the desires of the body are connected to the rational perceptions of the mind. She and Rearden desired each other because of their respect and admiration for each other.

In stark contrast to the passion Dagny and Rearden have shared, Jim and Lillian's encounter is tawdry and cheap. They are not motivated by respect or admiration, or even the desire for a moment's pleasure. They are drawn to each other by their need to destroy Rearden. The only words spoken between them is Jim's reference to Lillian as "Mrs. Rearden." Lillian is still married to Rearden and believes she can hurt him with her infidelity. Rearden, of course, is far beyond caring, but Lillian does not know that. Finally, the picture of Jim is now complete. He is, as Cherryl accuses him, a killer for the sake of killing. He is a nihilist, seeking and enjoying the destruction of others. Although the rest of the looters are motivated by the quest for power and money, Jim does not enjoy these things the way he enjoys destroying men of integrity. His desire to celebrate the Argentinean deal has less to do with the fortune he stands to make than with the prospect of Francisco's ruin. Throughout his life, he has been driven to destroy the strong, capable people around him. Unable to accomplish his goal, he has chosen Cherryl as a substitute, because she is easier to destroy.

In Cherryl Brooks, Rand presents a true victim. Cherryl endures a profound transformation, from worshipping the best in people and believing she has found it in Jim, to comprehending evil in its purest form. When she sees Jim laid bare as the killer he is, she finds herself trapped. Though Dagny can offer her a brief refuge from the evil, she has no form of escape, either from her marriage or ultimately from the society in which Jim's values prevail. Her suicide is her way out, just as withdrawal from the looters' world is the strikers' way out.

PART THREE, CHAPTERS V–VI

Copper shortages make repairs impossible for Taggart. Under the Unification Plan, crucial materials are diverted to businessmen with Washington influence. The problem worsens when, at the precise moment that they were to be nationalized, the mines and properties of d'Anconia copper are blown up, and Francisco and his best employees disappear.

Rearden's brother Philip asks him for a job, but Rearden refuses, since Philip has no useful skills. He is surprised at Philip's sudden interest. Later, the Wet Nurse also asks for a job, wanting to finally do something productive. Though Rearden would like to hire him, the laws will not allow it. The Wet Nurse warns Rearden that the Washington men are working on new restrictions and secretly bringing their own men into the mills.

Despite terrible conditions, the farmers of Minnesota have generated a huge wheat crop and need trains to carry it off. Dagny learns that Taggart's cars have been diverted by the corrupt Cuffy Meigs to Louisiana, where they are used to carry soybeans for an experimental project run by the mother of a politician. The cars cannot be rerouted in time, and the wheat crop rots, guaranteeing starvation for many. The farming businesses in Minnesota are all destroyed.

The traffic system in the Taggart terminal has short-circuited. While dealing with the emergency, Dagny sees John Galt among the workers. Later, she walks off into the tunnels. He follows, and they make passionate love. Afterwards, he tells her he has been watching her for ten years from these very tunnels. He warns her not to look for him. If she were to lead the looters to him, he might be killed.

Rearden's union steelworkers ask for a raise, but Rearden is never told. The Unification Board rejects their request. Later, the Board-controlled newspapers publish stories of the hardship of the steelworkers and the unfair denial of their raise, without mentioning who denied it. Later, Rearden receives notice that his accounts will be attached to pay for phony back taxes. He does nothing, waiting to see what the looters are up to. He receives a phone call from a bureaucrat named Tinky Holloway, who asks him to attend a meeting to straighten everything out. Rearden agrees to attend. Holloway believes Rearden is intractable, based on Philip Rearden's report on his recent visit to his brother.

Rearden's family summons him to the house and pleads with him not to disappear. He rejects their apologies and their cries for pity. By asking him to remain, they are asking him to sacrifice himself for them, and this is unforgivable to him. In a pathetic attempt to destroy him, Lillian confesses her infidelity with Jim, but Rearden is beyond caring. When his family points out that he cannot disappear without money, he realizes why the attachment orders were placed.

Rearden goes to the meeting to straighten out his situation. Jim Taggart, Wesley Mouch, and several other looters are also there. They inform Rearden that they are passing a Steel Unification Plan, designed to pool profits like the Railroad Plan. He replies that under the plan, Orren Boyle would make the bulk of profits and he would go bankrupt no matter how much steel he made. Rearden suddenly grasps the nature of their game. Their entire system is based on the knowledge that he will always continue working, at any cost, because he loves his work and he is good at it.

When Rearden returns to the mill, a riot begun by government thugs is already underway. The Wet Nurse has been shot after refusing to help the goons enter the mills. He dies in Rearden's arms. Rearden is hit on the head and collapses, but an unknown worker kills his attacker and organizes the workers to defend themselves. Later, Rearden learns this worker is Francisco d'Anconia, who has been secretly working in the mills since he destroyed d'Anconia Copper.

ANALYSIS: PART THREE, CHAPTERS V–VI

Rand sets up a contrast between the two job seekers who appeal to Rearden. His brother Philip expects a job because he is Rearden's brother and therefore his responsibility, at least in a society that endorses the idea that men are "their brother's keepers." But mostly Philip expects one because he claims to need it, and need is the only qualification a socialist society requires. Rearden is vehement in rejecting Philip's request and suspicious of his motives. His suspicion is warranted, as it is later revealed that Philip is a stooge for the looters. On the other end of the spectrum, when the Wet Nurse asks for a job, even as a menial laborer, he does so because he wants to produce instead of living off the producers. He has been transformed by his experience in the mills and has come to reject his earlier beliefs. In this respect, he is alone among the looters. Furthermore, he does not assume Rearden will simply give him a job.

The looters have traveled so far down the path of power and influence that they have lost sight of issues of life and death and cannot see beyond the moment. This fact is dramatically illustrated by the ruin of the wheat crop in Minnesota. The starvation that will result will kill many, but the looters fail to see the impact on themselves. Their short-sightedness is astonishing and deeply irrational. As long as they are able to maintain their power today, they are willing to risk tomorrow and allow society to return to a pre-industrial Dark Age. Believing they have Rearden right where they want him, the looters move in for the kill. Yet even as they seek to destroy his business (and prop up Orren Boyle's) with the Steel Unification Plan, they need him to continue to produce. The attachments to his accounts are designed to keep him from leaving by cutting off his access to money, but they don't know he has Danneskjold's gold. Besides, Rearden can no longer be touched. He is unaffected by the looters' efforts and by the appeals of his pathetic family. He is especially untouched by Lillian's confession of her infidelity with Jim. His lack of interest in the news negates her life's purpose of destroying him, and she is devastated.

The government-staged riot at Rearden's mills, like Project X, reveals the brute force supporting the looters' regime and finally allows Rearden to give up and join Francisco. The violence is designed to ease the way for a government takeover of the company, which would appear to be for Rearden's own protection. In the battle, the Wet Nurse is sacrificed, but at least he has fought on the side of good. After his death, Rearden is finished. He can no longer participate in the looters' world and lend his mind to their system. He is ready to join Francisco and the strikers. Francisco has always been Rearden's friend and protector, even when he appeared to be his enemy. Now, Rearden knows his instincts about Francisco have been right all along. Their friendship is based on shared values and mutual admiration and forms a model for the types of relationships Rand believed were possible in a truly rational world. Rearden and Francisco have something else in common as well. Both have loved Dagny—and both have lost her.

Part Three, Chapters VII–VIII

Summary — Chapter VII: "This is John Galt Speaking"

> *Centuries ago, the man who was — no matter what his errors — the greatest of your philosophers, has stated the formula defining the concept of existence and the rule of all knowledge: A is A. A thing is itself. You have never grasped the meaning of his statement. I am here to complete it: Existence is Identity, Consciousness is Identification.*
>
> (See QUOTATIONS, p. 70)

Rearden vanishes, sending Dagny a note that says only, "I have met him. I don't blame you." Without him, the output of the steel industry shrinks. The country is panicky, and violent gangs gain control. Newspapers tell conflicting stories, mostly in the form of denials, but everywhere the collapse of society is obvious.

In an attempt to calm the public, the government announces that Mr. Thompson, the Head of State, will give a speech on all stations to address the crisis. The date and time are announced repeatedly for a week. At the moment the speech is to begin, the airwaves are taken over, and John Galt addresses the public instead. Galt delivers a long, detailed speech about the state of the nation and the strike of the mind and its reasons.

He denounces the mystics who claim God as the highest moral authority, and the socialists, who claim one's neighbors as the highest moral authority. He argues that morality is not an arbitrary system imposed from the outside, but an integral part of man himself. Man's reason, Galt says, is his moral faculty. Serving himself is the highest goal of the moral man. He describes the principles under which every man must live: reason, purpose, and self-esteem. These principles, he declares, imply and require all of man's virtues: rationality, independence, integrity, honesty, justice, productiveness, and pride. He calls for a general strike, asking those with any shred of reason left to withdraw their sanction and stop supporting their own destroyers. He urges people to accept reality and to stop shrinking from knowledge, but accept it and reclaim the concept of an objective reality.

Summary—Chapter VIII: The Egoist

After the speech, Mr. Thompson and the other Washington men are terrified and desperate. Dr. Stadler suggests coldly that they should kill Galt. Mr. Thompson thinks that Galt is a man of action, precisely what the nation needs, and that he can get the retired industrialists back. Thompson wants to negotiate with him.

After the broadcast, Eddie tells Dagny that he knows John Galt, that for years he has talked to him at the Taggart cafeteria. He wonders if he was helping to save or to destroy the railroad. Dagny asks him to keep his knowledge of Galt's employment secret, because the government is desperate to find him.

The country falls deeper into chaos. The government searches for Galt, while a steady flow of broadcasts announce that John Galt will solve the country's problems. Thompson asks Dagny if she knows where to find Galt. He hints that the situation is now desperate. He can no longer control the government's dangerous faction, and if they were to find Galt first, they might kill him. She tells Thompson that she does not know where Galt is. After her conversation with Mr. Thompson, Dagny is so afraid for Galt that she rushes to his apartment. When she reaches him, he tells her that she was followed by government agents, and in a short time they will storm the apartment. He tells her that she must pretend to be against him. If they realize the nature of Galt and Dagny's relationship, they will use her to torture him. When the agents appear to arrest him, she pretends he is her enemy.

The looters hold Galt prisoner while they try to convince him to become the country's economic dictator, but he refuses. Since he is literally at gunpoint, he agrees to perform any task they tell him to do, but he refuses to think for them. His mind cannot be compelled. Several men attempt to convince him, appealing to his sense of pity, greed, or fear, but Galt is unbreakable. He asks to see Dr. Stadler, who is deeply shaken by the encounter. Meanwhile, the newspapers declare that Galt has decided to help the government and that he is currently conferring with the nation's leaders. No one on the street believes the articles, and most do not believe that Galt has been found at all. To reassure the people, the looters announce the unveiling of the John Galt Plan for the economy, but at a television appearance to announce it, Galt reveals to the cameras a hidden gun pointing at him. He says to the cameras, "Get the hell out of my way!"

Civil war breaks out in California, and the Comet is stranded. Eddie leaves to try to restore Taggart's transcontinental service.

Dagny receives a letter from Francisco telling her to contact him if Galt is in danger.

ANALYSIS: PART THREE, CHAPTERS VII–VIII

The John Galt speech, like Roark's speech in Rand's other major novel, *The Fountainhead,* forms the philosophical heart of the novel and the basis for much of Rand's philosophy. The central tenet is that reason, not faith or emotion, forms the basis of human prosperity. Men must choose the rational over the irrational and accept objective reality, since, as Galt says, existence exists ("A is A"). Furthermore, men must live for their own self-interest, pursuing their own values, and not for others. To do so, they must be free of any interference from the government or other institutions that might seek to enslave the mind. The mind, as the motive power of the world, must be free. Most of the ideas presented in the speech have appeared before, in pieces of conversations, but here they are integrated into a single, comprehensive statement. Galt's speech is an ultimatum for the men in power and a call to arms for their victims.

In believing Galt will negotiate with the government, the looters seriously miscalculate. Thompson assumes Galt can be tempted by power for its own sake. He imagines Galt will compromise his ideals in exchange for a role in the government. Dr. Ferris and Cuffy Meigs, meanwhile, understand that Galt is their enemy and that his position is not negotiable. If he is put in charge, the looters will no longer be able to exist. They see killing him as their only means of self-preservation, though they may be wrong to assume they will survive at all in the spiraling chaos that engulfs the country. Dr. Stadler agrees that Galt threatens his existence, and his meeting with Galt destroys what little remains of his self-worth. He has worked hard to avoid objective reality, and Galt makes the avoidance impossible. Stadler must confront what he has become and the world he is in, and this is more than he can bear. Where men like Stadler and Jim remain dark and unknown to themselves, Galt possesses the light of self-knowledge, which cannot help but illuminate everything. In the world of Rand's philosophy, nothing is more deadly to a creature of illusion and obscurity than light and clarity.

The clash between Galt and the looters is the battle of mind versus muscle. The looters have only brute force as a tool, while Galt has his mind. Although the looters can use force to command him physically, they are powerless to coerce his mind. The notion that they can compel him to think for them, in fact to want to think for them, is preposterous. Yet they cannot imagine a man so completely immune to compulsion and corruption that he would refuse to accept the power they offer him, even at gunpoint.

PART THREE: CHAPTERS IX–X

SUMMARY — CHAPTER IX: THE GENERATOR

Dr. Stadler realizes that whether or not Galt relents, Stadler no longer has a place in Washington. To carve out a position of power for himself, he drives to the site of Project X, hoping to seize control of the weapon, but he is too late. Cuffy Meigs has already arrived with the same idea. As they fight over control of the weapon, the weapon is detonated, and the countryside is destroyed for hundreds of miles in all directions.

The Washington men are unnerved and desperate. Dr. Ferris convinces them to try torturing Galt. Dagny hears their decision and telephones Francisco. Just as she is about to leave to meet him, a panicked engineer rushes into her office and tells her that the Taggart Bridge has been destroyed in the Project X disaster. For the first time, she does not try to fix the problem. When she meets Francisco, she solemnly recites Galt's oath to him. She is now on strike.

At the State Science Institute, Galt is tortured with a device called Project F, as Dr. Ferris, Wesley Mouch, and Jim Taggart look on. The device runs electrical currents through his body. Dr. Ferris tells him that he will not be allowed to leave the room until he provides a complete outline of the measures he intends to take as economic dictator. Galt endures the torture without speaking. When the machine breaks down, he tells the man operating it how to fix it. The operator realizes in horror what is happening and rushes out of the room. In his overwhelming desperation to see Galt destroyed, Jim finally realizes his true nature as a nihilist, and the knowledge is too much to bear. He screams and collapses.

SUMMARY — CHAPTER X: IN THE NAME OF THE BEST WITHIN US

The strikers—Dagny, Rearden, Francisco, and Danneskjold—rescue Galt in a dramatic gunfight. They climb aboard Francisco's airplane, which has been waiting outside, and fly toward Colorado.

The locomotive of the Comet, eastbound from San Francisco, breaks down in the middle of a desert in Arizona. The conductor informs Eddie Willers that the engineer is working on the problem, but the look of resignation in his eyes implies that nothing can be done. Eddie is angry and frustrated. He had worked relentlessly to restore service. He is bitterly determined to hold on to the railroad and his faith in the world. When the crew and passengers are rescued by a caravan of covered wagons, Eddie refuses to desert the train.

With the complete collapse of the looters' way of life, the residents of the valley are finally ready to return to the world and rebuild it according to their beliefs.

ANALYSIS: PART THREE, CHAPTERS IX–X

Stadler's death in the Project X disaster is perfect justice. Through his denial of the mind, he has embraced its opposite—brute force. In the end, he is no better than the thug Cuffy Meigs, who is also hoping to use the weapon to rule others. The weapon itself is the manifestation of the enslaved mind. It represents Stadler's mind, or more specifically, the science his mind produced, which has been harnessed to the machine's evil purpose. Having lived by the enslavement of the mind, it is only proper that Stadler should die by it as well.

Until now, Dagny has been the last holdout among the industrialists. She has continued to believe that the looters are willing to see reality, at least in terms of their own survival. Now she understands that they are willing to sacrifice everything in order to avoid facing the world they have made. Although they desperately need Galt and the mind he represents, even to repair the machine they torture him with, still they will risk his life and even kill him. Such willingness shows they have come to embrace death. The strikers were right all along, and she must now withdraw her mind. Her refusal to help with the Taggart Bridge disaster is her resignation.

The belief system embodied in John Galt and the striking industrialists is intensely important to Rand, as evidenced by the near-religious imagery in the novel's final scene. Galt's gesture is a benediction as he blesses the valley and the world to which they return with his most sacred symbol—a dollar sign drawn in the air.

IMPORTANT QUOTATIONS EXPLAINED

1. But what can you do when you have to deal with people?

This question is uttered on many occasions by Dr. Stadler, first in Part One, Chapter VII. The question demonstrates his and the looters' belief that people are generally irrational and must be dealt with in a manipulative or repressive manner. Stadler believes most people are incapable of rational thought and must be told what is best for them. He believes they will support pure thought only if it is government-sanctioned, and this is why he has supported the creation of the State Science Institute. As the story progresses, this view of people becomes a justification for the increasing power of the government and its adoption of brute force. The question is also stated by Dr. Floyd Ferris at the unveiling of Project X. While coercing Stadler to deliver his speech praising the monstrous machine, Ferris reminds him that at a time of hysteria, riots, and mass violence, the people must be kept in line by any means necessary. He underscores his message by quoting the question Stadler himself is known for asking.

2.   Contradictions do not exist. Whenever you think that you are facing a contradiction, check your premises. You will find that one of them is wrong.

Francisco says this to Dagny in Part One, Chapter VII, when she challenges him for squandering his talent as a worthless playboy. Dagny asks him how he can be such a paradox, how a man as capable, brilliant, and accomplished as he is can also choose to be a worthless playboy. It does not seem possible that he can be both, and yet he seems to be. In asking her to check her premises, Francisco suggests that it is indeed not possible. He cannot be both things at once, because contradictions cannot exist. A thing is what it is, not something else entirely. Therefore, there must be another answer that Dagny has not seen yet. Hugh Akston (who had been Francisco's teacher) says something similar to Dagny when she meets him at the diner where he works as a short-order cook. He tells her this in response to her disbelief over why a famous philosopher would choose to work in a diner, or why a motor with the power to revolutionize industry would be abandoned in ruins. He urges her to look beyond her assumptions in the search for an answer that could make sense.

3.   John Galt is Prometheus who changed his mind. After
      centuries of being torn by vultures in payment for having
      brought to men the fire of the gods, he broke his chains—
      and he withdrew his fire—until the day when men withdraw
      their vultures.

Francisco says this to Dagny in Part Two, Chapter V, after they discover the words "Who is John Galt?" scratched into a table at a res-
taurant. She says there are so many stories about him, and Francisco
tells her that all the stories are true. Metaphorically speaking, they
are, and Francisco's Prometheus story is especially apt. Prometheus
was a figure from Greek mythology. He was a titan who stole fire
from the gods and brought it to men to improve their lives. In return,
he was chained to a rock and tortured. Vultures ate his liver each
day, only to have it grow back at night to be eaten again. In Francisco's comment, Prometheus (personified by Galt) represents the
great industrialists who have provided men with prosperity and
improved their lives with their inventions and products, but have
received only condemnation and government interference in return.
These men, led by Galt, have disappeared and taken their prosper-
ity-generating minds (the "fire" they had provided) with them. They
will no longer allow themselves to receive torture as payment for
their talents, and they will only return their talents to the world
when they are no longer punished for bringing them.

4. I swear by my life and my love of it that I will never live for the sake of another man, nor ask another man to live for mine.

This is the oath the thinkers recite when they join the strike and come to live in the valley; we first encounter this oath in Part Three, Chapter I. No one may stay until he or she is willing to take the oath freely. Dagny first encounters it as an inscription on the building where Galt's motor is kept. The words are so powerful that the sound of Galt reciting them opens the locks of the building's door. When Dagny sees the inscription, she tells Galt this is already the code she lives by, but she does not think his way is the right way to practice the code. He tells her they will have to see which one of them is right. Later, when it is clear that Galt's way was right, Dagny solemnly recites the oath to Francisco in the Taggart Terminal just before they rescue Galt from the looters, in Part Three, Chapter IX. The striker's code presents Rand's belief in egoism, or the doctrine of rational self-interest. Rand believes that individuals have an inalienable right to pursue their own happiness based on their own values and that they must be free to pursue their own self-interest as they choose. Under this code, people have no obligations to each other beyond the obligation to respect the freedom and rights of other self-interested people.

5. Centuries ago, the man who was—no matter what his errors—the greatest of your philosophers, has stated the formula defining the concept of existence and the rule of all knowledge: A is A. A thing is itself. You have never grasped the meaning of his statement. I am here to complete it: Existence is Identity, Consciousness is Identification.

This passage is part of the radio broadcast delivered by John Galt to the people of America in Part Three, Chapter VII. The man he refers to is the ancient Greek philosopher Aristotle, whose work had a profound influence on Rand and her philosophy of Objectivism. The concept that A is A was put forth in Aristotle's Law of Identity, where he held that everything that exists has a specific nature and a single identity. A can only be A; it cannot also be B. For Galt (embodying Rand's philosophy), this means that things exist: they are what they are regardless of the nature of the observer. Even if a person wants A to be something else or believes it should be something else, it is still A. The work of a person's consciousness is to perceive reality in its objective sense, to identify and recognize it as what it is, not to invent an alternate reality. Galt and the thinkers he represents are rational and perceive the reality that is, while the looters try, through denial, coercion, and manipulation, to assert an alternate reality that cannot be.

KEY FACTS

FULL TITLE
Atlas Shrugged

AUTHOR
Ayn Rand

TYPE OF WORK
Novel

GENRE
Mystery; romance; epic; philosophy treatise

LANGUAGE
English

TIME AND PLACE WRITTEN
1946–1957; Unites States

DATE OF FIRST PUBLICATION
1957

PUBLISHER
Random House

NARRATOR
The story is told by an anonymous third-person narrator.

POINT OF VIEW
The narrator speaks in the third person, focusing mainly on Dagny and Rearden, but following all the characters. Characters and actions are described subjectively; the narrator offers insight into the inner emotions and thoughts of the characters as well as their outward activities.

TONE
On the surface, the story is narrated in a detached, objective tone, but Rand's underlying attitude toward modern society is bitterly ironic and satirical.

TENSE
Past

SETTING (TIME)

Unspecified point in the second half of the twentieth century

SETTING (PLACE)

The United States

PROTAGONIST

Dagny Taggart

MAJOR CONFLICT

Dagny must try to keep her railroad from collapsing before she can find the destroyer who is systematically removing the men of the mind from the world.

RISING ACTION

As the dangerous collectivist policies of powerful looters plunge the country into chaos and the destroyer claims more men, Dagny begins to doubt her commitment to the railroad.

CLIMAX

Dagny follows the destroyer, John Galt, and discovers the vanished men, who urge her to join their strike of the mind; she is torn between love for her railroad and the rationality of their position.

FALLING ACTION

The looters imprison Galt, revealing their true evil nature, and Dagny realizes she must join the strike; she and the other strikers rescue Galt in a gunfight.

THEMES

The importance of the mind; the evils of collectivism; the need to integrate mind and body

MOTIFS

Rhetorical questions; motive power; bridges

SYMBOLS

The sign of the dollar; the bracelet; Wyatt's Torch; Atlas

FORESHADOWING

Paul Larkin warns Rearden to watch his "Washington man," Wesley Mouch, who will rise to power after betraying Rearden and ultimately try to destroy Rearden Steel. Francisco describes his mismanagement of the San Sebastian Mines as the result of following politically popular ideas. Later, the large-scale destruction of the economy naturally follows from the looters' devotion to these ideas. Francisco warns the looters that their complex political and economic structure could be destroyed by someone's simply naming the exact nature of what they are doing. In his radio speech, Galt does just this.

Study Questions & Essay Topics

Study Questions

1. *What does Ayn Rand mean by "the sanction of the victim"? What does it mean when Rearden refuses to give it at his trial?*

The sanction of the victim is the willingness of the victim to accept the moral terms under which he or she is accused. This willingness allows the oppressor to coerce the victim through guilt and obligation. Rational people will withhold their sanction when they do not accept the premise under which they are victimized. If their own moral code is not the code of their oppressors, they are not obligated to participate under the oppressors' terms or to validate the oppressors' position by accepting it as rational. Under the collectivist system Rand describes in the novel, the producers are made to feel morally obligated to provide for those who do not produce but live off the products made by others. The system presents a morality of altruism in which all people are considered their brothers' keepers and the strong feel compelled to sacrifice themselves for the weak. To Rand, this system is fundamentally wrong. The only way a government can really force its people to sacrifice themselves is by brute force. When a rational person withdraws sanction and refuses to participate in his or her own victimization, the government can either resort to force or it must back down.

At his trial, Rearden does not accept the laws he has broken as rational, so he refuses to participate. He sees them as what they are: the manifestation of brute force. The government is able to prosecute him as a criminal only because they have created unjust laws that turn him into one. He withholds his sanction of the trial and makes it clear that the government must either compel him with violence or leave him alone. But the government cannot risk revealing the brute force that its power is based on, so it has no choice to but to let him go.

2. *Ayn Rand intended for* ATLAS SHRUGGED *to demonstrate her philosophy of Objectivism in action. How successful was she in showing how Objectivism can work in the real world?*

By presenting her philosophy in the format of a novel, Rand sought to demonstrate her principles at work in the actions of her characters and bring her philosophical concepts to life. Her efforts have mixed results. She succeeds in using her characters to explain the concepts of Objectivism. The messages are easier to understand in the context of a story than they might be in a straight philosophic treatise. Moreover, Rand does succeed in making her heroes embody the rationality and self-interest upon which her philosophy is based. The many speeches delivered by the strikers, most notably Francisco's "money speech" and Galt's lengthy radio address, are effective means of presenting ideas that might otherwise be too dry for many readers. But it seems unlikely that real people would speak this way, and the characters suffer as a result.

Rand's characterizations are absolute and hard to imagine in reality. The heroes are idealized and perhaps too perfect. Dagny, Rearden, Francisco, Galt, and Danneskjold are all physically attractive, astonishingly gifted, and possess tremendous personal integrity. Meanwhile the looters are all weak, evil, and irrational in every aspect. Only Cherryl Brooks and the Wet Nurse exist between these extremes, but they are tragic victims and minor characters. Furthermore, Rand's characters are free to devote themselves to their efforts, whether productive or parasitic, because none of them have to deal with children, illness, or any other issue that demands attention in the typical life. While they are effective as idealized representatives of Rand's ideas, the characters offer little for readers to identify with, making it difficult for them to imagine how Objectivism may apply to their own lives.

3. *How do events in* ATLAS SHRUGGED *support Ayn
   Rand's view that capitalism is the only moral economic
   system?*

Rand's argument in favor of capitalism is mostly illustrated through
her description of the failure of its alternatives. Rand demonstrates
how the self-sacrificing code of socialism ultimately creates an irrational system where need matters more than production. She highlights the government's interference in the economy and the fact that
every government action has unanticipated effects that in turn
require more intervention to fix. An example of the irrationality of
this system is the set of rules placed on Rearden that require him to
simultaneously limit his output of Rearden Metal and fill every
order he receives. Rand demonstrates that the logical outcome of
this spiraling interference is the government's Directive 10-289,
which is not only totalitarian but absurd. Furthermore, the seizing
of resources to serve "the needy" only makes those whose resources
have been seized become needy. When resources can be obtained
only by demonstrating the greatest need, as was the case at the
Twentieth Century Motor Company, the strong are enslaved by the
weak. By showing how socialism destroys productivity and domi-
nates individuals, Rand helps to promote capitalism as its antidote.

If, as Rand suggests, the notion of sacrifice for the "public good"
is the force behind the destruction of society, then only a system that
does not attempt to serve the public good can be moral—and only
unfettered capitalism meets this criteria. The strikers' code requires
a totally free exchange of goods and ideas in trades of "value for
value." Only capitalism can offer that freedom from intervention
and allow people to do business based on their own values. Therefore, for the strikers (and for Rand), capitalism is the only truly
moral economic system.

SUGGESTED ESSAY TOPICS

1. *What role does Eddie Willers play in the unfolding drama? What does his character say about the role of the common man in the world of Ayn Rand?*

2. *What are the causes of the Taggart Tunnel disaster?*

3. *Why is Rearden willing to support his family despite their attitude toward him? What causes his position to change?*

4. *Is the current economic and political system in this country more like Galt's ideal or the looters'?*

5. *According to Ayn Rand, selfishness is a moral and practical good. What does Rand mean by selfishness?*

6. *What does Francisco mean when he says, "The words 'to make money' hold the essence of human morality"?*

Review & Resources

Quiz

1. What kind of company does Dagny Taggart run?

   A. A steel mill
   B. An automobile manufacturing plant
   C. A transcontinental railroad
   D. An oil company

2. What does the rhetorical question "Who is John Galt?" express?

   A. Hopelessness and futility
   B. A joy of living on earth
   C. Fear of mysticism and religion
   D. A yearning for identity and self-definition

3. What does Hank Rearden invent?

   A. The secret of eternal youth
   B. A motor capable of drawing power from static electricity in the air
   C. An alloy lighter than steel and twice as strong
   D. A new kind of smelter for copper

4. Who is the most powerful man in Washington?

   A. Jim Taggart, president of the nation's largest railroad
   B. Wesley Mouch, head of the Bureau of Economic Planning and National Resources
   C. Hank Rearden, inventor of Rearden Metal
   D. Midas Mulligan, the nation's richest banker

5. Why did Lillian marry Hank Rearden?

    A. She wanted to destroy him
    B. She admired his great capacity to produce
    C. She wanted to defy her elitist, socially conscious
        parents
    D. She pitied him

6. Why do Dagny and Rearden drive to the Twentieth Century
    Motor Company?

    A. They have heard that something very significant once
        happened there
    B. They wish to find the owner and ask him to return to
        the world
    C. They need to purchase machine parts, which are
        quickly becoming impossible to find
    D. They know that it is the only truly worthwhile factory
        still in operation

7. How does Dagny find a good engineer to reconstruct the
    static engine?

    A. She hires a gaunt, intelligent man she meets on the
        street
    B. She goes to Robert Stadler for help
    C. She pays Rearden to send over one of his own engineers
    D. She hires a young man who calls himself John Galt

8. Why does Dagny become Galt's maid in the valley?

    A. She wants to pay off the damage she caused to his
        house
    B. Everyone must have a job in the valley
    C. She does not wish to use the bank account waiting for
        her in Mulligan Bank
    D. She wants to prove to Galt that she is domestically
        inclined

9. How does Rearden know Dagny has fallen in love with another man?

   A. When describing her relationship with Rearden over the radio, Dagny used only the past tense
   B. He smelled someone else's cologne on her
   C. He received a letter from Lillian informing her of Dagny's infidelity
   D. He secretly followed her into the valley

10. What is the intent of Directive 10-289?

    A. To freeze the economy in its current state
    B. To ease the government stranglehold on big business
    C. To bring John Galt to justice
    D. To eliminate competition from foreign companies

11. According to Francisco, what has replaced the Aristocracy of Money?

    A. The Aristocracy of Fraud
    B. The Kings of Comedy
    C. The Czar of the Bizarre
    D. The Aristocracy of Pull

12. Why did Francisco remain as head of d'Anconia Copper?

    A. He knew that Dagny would not forgive him if he quit
    B. He wished to save the company from ruin
    C. He had to deliberately destroy it, or it would stand for centuries
    D. He wanted to defy John Galt's strict code

13. Why is Eddie Willers troubled to see Rearden's robe in Dagny's apartment?

    A. He thought that Rearden had long ago disappeared
    B. He has been in love with Dagny for years
    C. He knows that Dagny is now John Galt's lover
    D. Rearden is an outspoken opponent of marital infidelity

14. What formula does Ragnar Danneskjold use to determine how much to deposit in his accounts for the victimized industrialists?

   A. The amount of money they will need to rebuild their companies after the strike
   B. The total sum of the taxes they paid to the federal government
   C. Their relative moral worth
   D. The losses they took under Directive 10-289

15. Why is the John Galt Line closed down?

   A. Its strong new rail is needed to patch up a transcontinental line
   B. Many clients and investors are afraid that Rearden Metal will not be able to support the weight of a freight train
   C. Dagny's retirement destroys Taggart Transcontinental
   D. The Taggart Bridge collapses, and the company desperately needs Rearden Metal to rebuild it

16. What job has John Galt been doing all along?

   A. Furnace foreman at Rearden Steel
   B. Track laborer for Taggart
   C. Thug at the State Science Institute
   D. Cook at a small diner

17. Which ships does Ragnar Danneskjold sink?

   A. Those that carry foreign aid supplies stolen from America's industrialists
   B. Those that do not fly a triangular white flag
   C. Those that carry pure gold
   D. Those that have never participated in war

18. Why did Richard Halley quit?

   A. His most beloved concerto was a failure
   B. Society only accepted his work because he had suffered
   C. He spotted John Galt watching one of his operas
   D. He could no longer find inspiration in a corrupt world

19. What is the Wet Nurse's real name?

    A. Tony
    B. Frank Adams
    C. Hayes
    D. His name is never revealed

20. Who is John Galt?

    A. A brilliant inventor who accidentally inspired a revolution when he quit the Twentieth Century Motor company
    B. Eddie's grease-stained cafeteria friend
    C. The destroyer
    D. All of the above

21. How does Mr.Thompson find John Galt?

    A. Dagny makes an angry phone call
    B. Robert Stadler suggests he have Dagny followed
    C. Wesley Mouch devises a scheme
    D. An ambitious young radio engineer traces the source of Galt's broadcast

22. How does the Ferris Persuader work?

    A. By torturing the subject with sharp, random bursts of electricity
    B. By stripping the subject of resistance through a recently discovered chemical agent
    C. By invoking the subject's pity with hundreds of pictures of human suffering
    D. By pure illusion, impressing in the subject a great, unfounded fear of torture

23. What does Jim Taggart finally realize he is motivated by?

    A. The desperate need to destroy greatness
    B. A sick, twisted pity for others
    C. Pure, blind greed for unearned money
    D. An unconfessed lust for his sister Dagny

24. Which of Halley's concertos is played throughout the strikers' valley?

    A.   His Third Concerto
    B.   His Fourth Concerto
    C.   His Fifth Concerto
    D.   His Sixth Concerto

25. Why does John Galt address the nation on the radio?

    A.   He wants to explain the strike
    B.   He wants to announce the availability of his motor
    C.   He has accepted the job of Economic Dictator
    D.   He is running for office

SUGGESTIONS FOR FURTHER READING

BERLINER, MICHAEL, ed. *Letters of Ayn Rand*. Transl. by Dina Garmong. New York: Dutton, 1995.

BINSWANGER, HARRY, ed. *The Ayn Rand Lexicon: Objectivism from A to Z*. New York: New American Library, 1986.

HARRIMAN, DAVID, ed. *The Journals of Ayn Rand*. New York: Plume, 1997.

PEIKOFF, LEONARD. *Objectivism: The Philosophy of Ayn Rand*. New York: Meridian, 1993.

———, ed. *The Voice of Reason: Essays in Objectivist Thought*. New York: Meridian, 1990.

RAND, AYN. *Capitalism: The Unknown Ideal*. New York: New American Library, 1967.

———. *The Fountainhead*. Indianapolis: Bobbs-Merrill, 1943.

———. *The New Left: The Anti-Industrial Revolution*. New York: Signet, 1971.

———. *The Virtue of Selfishness: A New Concept of Egoism*. New York: New American Library, 1964.

SPARKNOTES TEST PREPARATION GUIDES

The SparkNotes team figured it was time to cut standardized tests down to size. We've studied the tests for you, so that SparkNotes test prep guides are:

Smarter
Packed with critical-thinking skills and test-
taking strategies that will improve your score.

Better
Fully up to date, covering all new features of the tests,
with study tips on every type of question.

Faster
Our books cover exactly what you need to
know for the test. No more, no less.

SparkNotes Literature Guides

1984
The Adventures of
    Huckleberry Finn
The Aeneid
All Quiet on the
    Western Front
And Then There Were
    None
Angela's Ashes
Animal Farm
Anna Karenina
Anne of Green Gables
Anthem
Antony and Cleopatra
As I Lay Dying
As You Like It
Atlas Shrugged
The Awakening
The Autobiography of
    Malcolm X
The Bean Trees
The Bell Jar
Beloved
Beowulf
Billy Budd
Black Boy
Bless Me, Ultima
The Bluest Eye
Brave New World
The Brothers
    Karamazov
The Call of the Wild
Candide
The Canterbury Tales
Catch-22
The Catcher in the Rye
The Chocolate War
The Chosen
Cold Mountain
Cold Sassy Tree
The Color Purple
The Count of Monte
    Cristo
Crime and Punishment
The Crucible
Cry, the Beloved
    Country
Cyrano de Bergerac
David Copperfield
Death of a Salesman
The Death of Socrates

The Diary of a Young
    Girl
A Doll's House
Don Quixote
Dr. Faustus
Dr. Jekyll and Mr. Hyde
Dracula
Dune
Edith Hamilton's
    Mythology
Emma
Ethan Frome
Fahrenheit 451
Fallen Angels
A Farewell to Arms
Farewell to Manzanar
Flowers for Algernon
For Whom the Bell
    Tolls
The Fountainhead
Frankenstein
The Giver
The Glass Menagerie
Gone With the Wind
The Good Earth
The Grapes of Wrath
Great Expectations
The Great Gatsby
Grendel
Gulliver's Travels
Hamlet
The Handmaid's Tale
Hard Times
Harry Potter and the
    Sorcerer's Stone
Heart of Darkness
Henry IV, Part I
Henry V
Hiroshima
The Hobbit
The House of Seven
    Gables
I Know Why the Caged
    Bird Sings
The Iliad
Inferno
Inherit the Wind
Invisible Man
Jane Eyre
Johnny Tremain
The Joy Luck Club

Julius Caesar
The Jungle
The Killer Angels
King Lear
The Last of the
    Mohicans
Les Miserables
A Lesson Before Dying
The Little Prince
Little Women
Lord of the Flies
The Lord of the Rings
Macbeth
Madame Bovary
A Man for All Seasons
The Mayor of
    Casterbridge
The Merchant of Venice
A Midsummer Night's
    Dream
Moby Dick
Much Ado About
    Nothing
My Antonia
Narrative of the Life of
    Frederick Douglass
Native Son
The New Testament
Nicomachean Ethics
Night
Notes from
    Underground
The Odyssey
The Oedipus Plays
Of Mice and Men
The Old Man and the
    Sea
The Old Testament
Oliver Twist
The Once and Future
    King
One Day in the Life of
    Ivan Denisovich
One Flew Over the
    Cuckoo's Nest
One Hundred Years of
    Solitude
Othello
Our Town
The Outsiders
Paradise Lost

A Passage to India
The Pearl
The Picture of Dorian
    Gray
Poe's Short Stories
A Portrait of the Artist
    as a Young Man
Pride and Prejudice
The Prince
A Raisin in the Sun
The Red Badge of
    Courage
The Republic
Richard III
Robinson Crusoe
Romeo and Juliet
The Scarlet Letter
A Separate Peace
Silas Marner
Sir Gawain and the
    Green Knight
Slaughterhouse-Five
Snow Falling on Cedars
Song of Solomon
The Sound and the Fury
Steppenwolf
The Stranger
Streetcar Named
    Desire
The Sun Also Rises
A Tale of Two Cities
The Taming of the
    Shrew
The Tempest
Tess of the d'Ubervilles
Their Eyes Were
    Watching God
Things Fall Apart
The Things They
    Carried
To Kill a Mockingbird
To the Lighthouse
Tom Sawyer
Treasure Island
Twelfth Night
Ulysses
Uncle Tom's Cabin
Walden
War and Peace
Wuthering Heights
A Yellow Raft in Blue
    Water